THE MISSING PEACE

THE MISSING PEACE

How to Be Held Together When You're Falling Apart

TIM ROSS

Bestselling Author of
Welcome to the Basement

NELSON BOOKS
An Imprint of Thomas Nelson

The Missing Peace
Copyright © 2026 by Tim Ross

Published by Nelson Books, an imprint of Thomas Nelson, 501 Nelson Place, Nashville, TN 37214, USA. Nelson Books and Thomas Nelson are registered trademarks of HarperCollins Christian Publishing, Inc.

Thomas Nelson titles may be purchased in bulk for educational, business, fundraising, or sales promotional use. For information, please email SpecialMarkets@ThomasNelson.com.

All emphasis in Scripture quotations is added by the author.

ISBN 978-1-4002-5434-7 (ITPE)

HarperCollins Publishers, Macken House, 39/40 Mayor Street Upper, Dublin 1, D01 C9W8, Ireland (https://www.harpercollins.com)

Library of Congress Cataloging-in-Publication Data

Names: Ross, Tim (Pastor), author.
Title: The missing peace: how to be held together when you're falling apart / Tim Ross, bestselling author of Welcome to the Basement.
Description: [Nashville, Tennessee]: Nelson Books, [2025] | Includes bibliographical references. | Summary: "In The Missing Peace, podcaster and thought leader Tim Ross introduces a stunning perspective on the peace Jesus left us to help us regulate our bodies and emotions as we break free of temporary happiness and walk toward freedom"—Provided by publisher.
Identifiers: LCCN 2025005162 (print) | LCCN 2025005163 (ebook) | ISBN 9781400247790 (hardcover) | ISBN 9781400247806 (ebook)
Subjects: LCSH: Peace of mind—Religious aspects—Christianity. | Resilience (Personality trait)—Religious aspects—Christianity.
Classification: LCC BV4908.5 .R673 2025 (print) | LCC BV4908.5 (ebook) | DDC 248.4—dc23/eng/20250721
LC record available at https://lccn.loc.gov/2025005162
LC ebook record available at https://lccn.loc.gov/2025005163

Art direction and cover design: Curt Diepenhorst
Interior design: Sara Guild

Printed in the United States of America

26 27 28 29 30 LBC 5 4 3 2 1

This book is for the mental health professionals—the real ones. The ones who didn't just help me survive my trauma but gave me the tools to thrive despite it. Y'all do holy work, and I'm living proof of it.

I also dedicate this book to Juliette, my daddy Charles, my mommy Maxinne, Korey and Sara Miller, Dr. Bobby Gibson, Nicole McAnn, Nancy Houston, and Brian and Stephanie Simmons. Y'all have seen me at my absolute worst and still helped me be my best. My memory ain't short, and my love for you runs deep.

Thank you. For real.

I love you,

Timothy

CONTENTS

FOREWORD

For over a decade I have watched Tim Ross evolve steadily and faithfully as a man of God, husband, father, son, servant leader, and relentless God-chaser. In recent years, however, I have watched him surrender his life and will in the quiet obedience that few ever see. His integrity, humility, and submission to God's plan are not only uncommon but worth studying. His aim for people to experience being fully seen, fully heard, fully known, and fully loved is clearly expressed and carefully detailed in his uncle-next-door tone.

It is through this unique lens that I have personally benefited from his emotional intelligence, Biblical literacy, and theological eloquence. Despite being misunderstood and publicly criticized, Tim continues to bear fruit, producing powerful, transformative works like this one. This level of insight comes only after a heart is surrendered and resolved to do the courageous work of intentional healing.

As a clinical pastoral caregiver and advocate for survivors of sexual and gender-based violence, I've spent over two decades walking alongside individuals, couples, and families—many of them carrying deep wounds from various trauma. I have been on my own healing journey since I was a teen and a helping professional since my twenties. Having engaged with a vast spectrum of healers—from therapists and spiritual directors to holistic wellness professionals—as a client, colleague, and trainer, I can say with full confidence: This book is a balm for the Body. It is an open-handed gift to individuals contemplating their healing journey, a great resource for nonclinical helping professionals, and a bridge for clinicians working with clients from diverse faith traditions.

Some authors write with a narrow focus or linear illustrations of wellness. This is not that. This book is a loving invitation to draw closer to God and embrace your most authentic self. It speaks to everyone navigating real-life experiences—those who long for the abundant life promised in John 10:10 yet find themselves stuck in survival mode. Tim bridges that gap, showing that the fullness Jesus promised includes the restoration of our minds and emotions. Because the language is unthreatening and accessible, the path forward feels attainable for every reader.

Throughout my experience, I have observed that many high-functioning adults are convinced that therapeutic support is unessential. Commonly, people who've experienced hardship pathologize their pain, internalizing it as proof that they are somehow defective. Strongly held cultural norms—especially in churches—maintain the conviction that therapy is only for those with extreme traumas or that faith alone should be sufficient to navigate hardship. Meanwhile, lives are wrought with emotional injuries that impact relationships, health, and callings. I firmly believe the lack of emphasis on emotional health has hindered our capacity for true transformation.

But if you fully engage this book, you will be liberated from those limiting beliefs. You will begin to make sense of your own coping strategies and patterns, realizing that your reactions to life's hardships are not pathological—they are human.

Tim Ross joins the chorus of faithful thought leaders who recognize the necessity of tending to the soul. By sharing his personal experience with various therapeutic modalities, he normalizes support through a faith-based lens. This is a revolutionary act. If you apply these suggestions, you are disrupting cycles of harm and strengthening the world around you.

As I read through this book, I felt witnessed, affirmed, and loved. So take your time. Sit with each chapter. Reflect, wrestle, respond, and pray. Digging into the wisdom offered here is your act of resistance. You will uncover your personal blueprint for wellness and deliverance. You are in the right place, with the right text, for this season of your life.

Rev. Dr. Sarai Crain
Pastoral leader, mental health practitioner, and advocate for survivors of sexual and gender-based violence

Introduction

SOMETHING AIN'T RIGHT

You know that moment in a movie when something seems to be going wrong but you're just not sure what it is? The hero approaches a seemingly harmless door, but the ominous music in the background alerts you that trouble is near. That's precisely the kind of twilight-zone vibe it feels like the world has been trapped in for years. Sure, we could endlessly debate about what's wrong with humanity, but honestly I think the pandemic and the surrounding years took a significant toll on most of us.

It feels as if around 2020 we hit a kind of time warp. Have you ever experienced something so profound or impactful that the years afterward either vanished entirely or blurred together, as if life were playing on fast-forward while you stood frozen? I glanced down for a moment to catch my breath and looked back up wondering, *It hasn't really been that long . . . has it?*

Something about the pandemic seemed to reset our perception of time. As if Thanos had snapped us into oblivion. (Sorry, not sorry—I'm a nerd, and we embrace nerdiness here. Hope you can roll with it!) The initial quarantine year and everything just afterward felt like the fictional Marvel Cinematic Universe snap. We gradually returned to consciousness and realized chaos had quietly erupted all around us.

In an alarmingly brief span, we became alienated from one another, confined indoors with our personal triggers and struggles. Wars threatened or erupted outright, global elections became explosive, racism surged anew on the historical roller coaster, unemployment soared alongside skyrocketing inflation, and our economies plunged. Even spiritual leaders, the pastors we trusted to maintain moral clarity amid chaos, started abandoning their posts like frightened sailors jumping ship.

Around 2020 it's like a global timer buzzed. In a kitchen a timer typically signals something good: *Ding!* Roast is ready! *Ding!* Cookies are done! *Ding!* Dinnertime!

But we weren't prepared cooks. Instead, our metaphorical oven caught fire. The glass we mistook for water and threw onto the flames turned out to be oil, turning our kitchen into an inferno.

And our reaction?

"You okay?" "Yep!" (*No! I'm an anxious mess.*)

"Everything good?" "Sure!" (*No way! Help! I'm depressed.*)

"How are you?" "Blessed and highly favored!" (*But my kids are out of control, my house is chaotic, and my job feels like it's collapsing! I'm screaming inside, but no one hears me!*)

If this hits a nerve, know you're not alone. Many of us aren't doing nearly as well as we pretend. According to the World Health Organization, anxiety and depression surged 25 percent globally in the first pandemic year.[1] In Finland, ADHD diagnoses jumped 18 percent during the pandemic, in a nation known for its ideal educational system.[2]

Meanwhile, loneliness quietly became an epidemic: Roughly half of US adults reported frequent loneliness during the pandemic, and even now 30 percent say they feel lonely at least once a week.[3]

Look around—this isn't just your story. Something serious is unfolding, and it's okay to admit we've been deeply shaken. After a year confined at home without distractions, it became clear who needed a therapist, psychiatrist, or divine intervention. Perhaps one silver lining of 2020 was that it forced us to stop fleeing ourselves and face our reality: that nobody is genuinely "fine." And let's be honest—"fine" is relative. Some people have normalized dysfunction, chaos, or emotional numbness as their version of fine because they've lived with it for so long. They've adjusted to discomfort as if it were comfort, to pain as if it were normal, to chaos as if it were peace. Recognizing this truth is crucial because only when we acknowledge that our definition of "fine" may not actually be healthy can we begin to seek healing and wholeness.

We're hurting—genuinely hurting. Anxiety grips us, relentless and unyielding. Depression weighs us down, a shadow that's always present. This isn't conjecture; it's the truth of our lives today. Deep within each of us is an agitation we can't quite name, a disquiet we struggle to resolve or even fully understand. It keeps us restless, searching, unsettled. And how do we cope? We smother this discomfort with distractions—shopping binges, endless gaming marathons, workaholism, substance abuse, excessive drinking, or pornography. Anything that numbs the pain, even briefly, seems worth the escape. Like frightened children trembling under blankets, we pretend our nightmares aren't real: "If I can't see it, maybe it won't see me." But beneath the blankets we're still afraid. The monsters haven't vanished—they're simply waiting, patiently, for the cover to slip.

So we remain scared, continuously running or hiding.

A friend once told me about a break-in at his home in Atlanta. His reflection shook me deeply. He shared, "When I returned, things had been moved around, cushions misplaced. Realizing someone had invaded my home was unsettling. But the most valuable thing they stole wasn't my TV or gadgets—it was my peace of mind. I slept with the lights on, constantly fearing they'd return."

That resonated deeply. After more than two decades in therapy, I've realized something crucial: Wealth, advanced security systems, dream cars, or perfect careers don't guarantee peace of mind. Consider Michael Jackson, widely acclaimed as the King of Pop, whose life seemed to embody everything we equate with ultimate success. He had global fame, vast wealth, unrivaled influence, and countless adoring fans. Yet, tragically, none of these accomplishments could bring him lasting inner peace. Despite his outward success, he struggled profoundly with anxiety and insomnia, ultimately relying on medical-grade anesthesia just to sleep.[4]

His heartbreaking death was a stark reminder that external validation and material possessions can never satisfy the deeper human need for peace. We've watched this play out repeatedly among celebrities and public figures, a sobering reality check for us all. If we think that winning the lottery, marrying the perfect partner, or landing our dream job will finally grant us lasting contentment, Michael's story reminds us otherwise. True peace requires something deeper—something that transcends fame, fortune, and accolades.

Clearly, something significant is missing.

We've chased countless dreams and pursued endless achievements, hoping each new accomplishment would finally deliver the peace and satisfaction we've longed for. Yet, despite our best efforts and greatest successes, the emptiness remains, persistent and unresolved. It's as though we're searching for a crucial piece of a puzzle without even knowing what the finished picture should look like.

Here's the good news: You don't have to stay stuck in that unsettling uncertainty or lingering emptiness. Perhaps you're not yet sure what's missing or exactly where to find it. But simply recognizing that there is something missing—and being willing to seek answers—is a powerful first step. Your curiosity and courage in facing this truth are already putting you on the path toward the peace you're seeking.

Here's how we'll navigate this journey together.

First, we'll spend some time establishing foundational insights and understandings. These chapters will set the stage for the deeper exploration ahead, offering you essential perspectives to help you engage effectively with what's to come. If you begin to feel stirred or unsettled in these early chapters, please know that's normal and even beneficial—it's a sign that you're engaging authentically with your own heart and mind. Hold tight, because the journey will be worth it.

Next, we'll enter the heart of the matter. Think of this stage as emotional heart surgery. We'll carefully and intentionally explore why the change you seek is so important, what the benefits are, and why pursuing this peace is worth the effort.

Finally, we'll shift our focus to practical, actionable steps toward achieving genuine freedom and lasting peace. You'll find clear strategies, encouraging guidance, and realistic insights that will support your continued growth and healing.

Throughout this process, know you're not alone. Whether you're reading this curled up on your sofa or listening to it while navigating daily life, we're walking this journey together. You don't have to have all the answers right now—just a willingness to keep moving forward, step by thoughtful step.

Before we dive deeper, a few disclaimers and trigger warnings.

If you've listened to *The Basement* or *Wide Open* podcasts or read *Welcome to the Basement*, this reminder might sound familiar: The content here isn't TMI (too much information); it's T-I-M—me being transparent. The topics and experiences I share in this book may evoke strong emotions. You might feel anger, fear, anxiety, sadness, guilt, confusion, or even resistance. These reactions are natural and valid. If my words provoke any of these emotions, I encourage you to explore inwardly first. Emotions like anger or fear tend to direct us outward toward the perceived source of discomfort, but curiosity leads us inward, facilitating healing and self-discovery. Whatever arises, let curiosity—not reactivity—guide your journey.

This book delves deeper into traumatic experiences than other books you may have read. Perhaps you've already been on your own healing journey, or maybe this is your first time diving this deep into sensitive topics. If that's the case, I want you to know it's completely understandable if parts of this book feel challenging or even overwhelming. This might not be the kind of book you curl up with to casually enjoy—some chapters and sections may feel particularly difficult. Please take breaks as needed; grab your favorite ice cream, stream your favorite show, or step away to breathe and recharge. Taking breaks is healthy and encouraged.

But here's the crucial part: If you abandon this journey completely or finish without experiencing meaningful change, that's okay. We're all wrestling with something, and this book is merely a starting point to help you acknowledge and address that reality. Therapy, in some form, is often essential. And while therapy frequently involves working with a licensed professional, it can also start with talking openly with a parent, sibling, trusted friend, counselor, coworker, or spiritual adviser. Sometimes the very act of speaking about our struggles can begin profound healing. Therapy transformed my life, and it might transform yours too. Wherever you decide to start—whether diving in headfirst or just dipping your toe in—your healing matters.

This book isn't exclusively for Christians. While my personal faith is deeply rooted in Jesus and my experiences reflect that, I acknowledge that readers may come from a variety of spiritual or life backgrounds. My goal is to communicate openly and authentically from my own journey while providing insights that anyone can relate to, regardless of where they stand spiritually. Throughout this book you'll find Scripture thoughtfully paired with practical wisdom and insights drawn from various reliable fields of study and lived experiences, making this exploration accessible and relevant for everyone.

Finally, therapists: My deepest heartfelt gratitude goes to you. I would not be who I am today without your profound dedication and care. Your tireless commitment has not only changed my life but shaped it in ways beyond measure. This book is not an attempt to step into your role—rather, it's a direct reflection of your meaningful work. I'm able to offer these insights and encouragements because you have faithfully and skillfully paved the way. Your profession's contributions have made this possible, and for that I am forever indebted. I proudly consider myself one of your greatest beneficiaries. Many people simply need validation that it's okay to acknowledge brokenness and pursue healing, and your work has always championed this truth. You pushed me so that I could push others.

Readers? Consider this your gentle push. I love you.

Holy Spirit, heal our minds. In Jesus's name, amen.

Let's go!

PART 1

BREAK THE SILENCE

1

WHAT AM I MISSING?

I think we can all agree—2020 was strange. Like, twilight-zone strange. The kind of year where reality itself seemed to take a left turn and never look back. It wasn't just the pandemic. It was the quarantine, the racial tension, the economic collapse, the mental health free fall, the political chaos—and all of it happening at the same time. A single one of those would've been enough to shake us. We got hit with all of them. And that collective weight? It was crushing.

I don't think we've fully processed what it meant to live through that year. I mean, pick one: a global pandemic that locked us indoors, decimated families, and sparked uncertainty about every cough, every doorknob, every decision. Racial tension was at an all-time high, with protests stretching from Minneapolis to Milan. And don't even get me started on that election. If you weren't exhausted by the headlines, the hashtags, or the heated Thanksgiving-dinner arguments, you probably weren't paying attention. We were in survival mode, all of us—our nervous systems fried, our spiritual rhythms fractured, our emotional capacity hanging by a thread.

Some of us were trapped in homes that didn't feel safe. Some of us were working from bedrooms, teaching kids algebra from iPads, while our hearts were in survival mode. Church services moved to live streams, but our souls still felt unplugged. Every headline felt like a threat. Every conversation felt charged. We weren't just missing structure. We were missing peace. And most of us didn't even realize how badly until it was gone.

But for me? Man, 2019 made 2020 look like a sabbatical. In 2020, when the rest of the world was stockpiling toilet paper, learning how to unmute Zoom, and riding the pandemic roller coaster, I was already in free fall. It's wild to even say it out loud, but if God gave me a choice to relive one of those years, I'd pick 2020. No hesitation. That's how brutal 2019 was for me.

THE IMPACT OF LOSS

I had been leading Embassy City Church for four years at that point, and from the outside things looked blessed—full services, expanding reach, all the right metrics trending up. But internally? I was cracking. That year, 2019, was the year that broke me the most. While the world was bracing for a global shake-up in 2020, my personal earthquake had already hit. And I was deep in the aftershocks before the world ever locked down.

Eight people I loved died that year. Eight. And three of them weren't just close—they were family in everything but blood. I don't even think you can rank that kind of pain. Loss isn't a competition, and it doesn't scale neatly. Every one of those deaths carved something out of me. But if I had to name the one that hit me the hardest—the one that destabilized me in ways I still feel—it was Kimmy.

Kimmy wasn't just my assistant. She was the internal compass that kept my life pointed north. She was my scheduler, my shield, my steady. She knew where I needed to be before I even asked. She reminded me who I needed to be when I was too tired to remember. She didn't just manage my calendar; she managed my pace. For seven years she literally ran my life, and she did it with the precision of a surgeon and the loyalty of family. From diagnosis to Kimmy's death, we had six months. GI cancer doesn't play fair, and it doesn't move slow. One minute we were doing life together—emails, appointments, reminders, laughter—and the next we were navigating hospice.

Her absence left a crater. I've tried to describe it before, but words don't always stretch far enough. So let me try it this way: Imagine losing your phone. Now multiply that by the panic, the confusion, the lack of direction you feel. Now imagine that phone wasn't just your lifeline—it was smarter than Siri, quicker than a Google search, more comforting than any playlist. That was Kimmy. She was my clarity in chaos, and losing her disoriented me in ways I still can't explain. Even now there are days I reach for her in my memory like I'm reaching for a phone I forgot I no longer carry.

While my heart was cracking, the church was growing. Fast. We doubled in size in a matter of months. On paper that looked like a win—a pastor's dream, even. From the outside it was everything we said we wanted: momentum, favor, impact. But from the inside I knew I was carrying it all wrong. I wasn't just tired—I was unraveling. From the way I was leading, I felt like I should fire myself.

The pressure wasn't about positions—it was about the pain. And I don't mean emotional pain like a vague sense of sadness. I mean the kind of weight that sits on your chest and makes every breath feel like a negotiation. I was in a monthly process group (a structured gathering with others led by a therapist to process emotions safely). I had a therapist. I had community. I had safe spaces to grieve. And it was still almost unbearable. I didn't have to hide my tears or appear to be perfect. I could be honest. And still—it was suffocating.

So I started thinking: *If I'm barely making it with all of this support, what about the people out here who have no support at all?* No therapist. No community. No space to process or even cry without judgment. No structure around them that says, "You're allowed to fall apart here."

How do you survive that? How do you not break when you're carrying that weight in silence? It's no wonder so many people don't make it through. This pressure will crush you if it doesn't have a place to go. And most people have nowhere to put it.

TIME TO DISAPPEAR

I want to say this with care, especially for the lead pastors out there—especially the ones who are bivocational like my parents were. I see you. I honor the way you stretch every dollar, every hour, and every ounce of energy to serve your people. I was in full-time ministry, but I wasn't immune to the illusion that I could do it all. And that illusion was costing me.

So I found a place to disappear. I wasn't trying to feel something else—I was trying not to feel anything at all. Gaming became that space for me. It wasn't about numbing; it was about distracting. I needed something to transport me out of my emotions, out of my body, out of that year. And PlayStation 4 became the portal.

I started gaming. Hard.

I wasn't gambling. No cards, no dice. Just my PlayStation 4. I escaped a world where I was expected to manage grief, solve problems, lead people, and hold it all together into one where all I had to do was hold a controller.

In that world, I was in control. If something went wrong,

I could restart. If I died, I respawned. If I failed, I had infinite chances. If I didn't like where the story was headed, I could quit the game or try a different one. There were no funerals, no eulogies, no hard conversations. Everything I couldn't fix in real life I could win, reroute, or pause in the game.

It gave me the illusion of peace—and, for a while, I bought into it. It wasn't just about not feeling pain. It was about feeling power. Gaming gave me a world where nothing could touch me unless I let it. So I made sure to place myself in front of that console every moment I could—after work, after church, whenever the day gave me a sliver of escape. But my sons, Nathan and Noah, were paying attention. At eleven and nine, they went to their mom, Juliette, and said, "Mommy, Daddy doesn't pay attention to us."

Hearing that wrecked me. It wasn't one of those moments when I could defend myself or push back. I knew they were right. Instantly. It was like a dagger straight through my heart, not because they were being harsh, but because they were being honest. That kind of truth from your own kids doesn't leave you the same.

In that moment I realized I had traded the peace of God for the illusion of peace from my PS4. So I packed it up. Custom paddles, fancy headset, travel case, and all—gone. I gave it away. Gaming wasn't inherently wrong. It had helped me cope for a season. But now it had become the thing that was keeping me from what mattered most.

Giving it away wasn't punishment. It was realignment. Soon after, I found myself more present—laughing freely with Juliette and fully engaging with Nathan and Noah over family dinners. Real peace felt lighter than I'd remembered. That act helped me recenter—come back to what peace actually looked like. And it helped me start showing up again for the people who matter most to me.

There's nothing wrong with a PS4—but I needed peace forevermore. I was missing peace. I was trying to fill that God-sized space with anything I could reach, and for a while that controller in my hand felt like enough. But it wasn't. It never could be. Not when what I truly longed for was lasting peace—the kind that doesn't glitch, pause, or need a reset button.

Here's the thing: I'm not the only one who's done this. We all put things in the God-sized hole inside us. We put work there. Sex. Anger. Hustle. Fear. Netflix. Porn. Perfectionism. Religion. Food. Anxiety. Control. Even happiness.

Yeah, I said it. Even happiness. Because happiness isn't peace.

We say we want happiness—and sure, it's nice—but that doesn't satisfy the real craving underneath. What we're after is peace. Happiness can be a fleeting feeling, a momentary high, a surface-level smile that can vanish with a phone call or a news alert. Peace is different. Peace is that soul-deep rest that holds you steady even when everything else is shaky. Happiness might come with a price tag, but peace? Peace is priceless. It can't be bought, borrowed, or hustled for. It's the kind of gift that doesn't make sense to the world and can't be explained in a spreadsheet—it just settles in your spirit and says, "You're safe now."

True peace can't be manufactured. It can't be achieved. It can only be given.

Paul said it best: True peace surpasses our understanding (Phil. 4:7). It doesn't make sense. It isn't logical. It doesn't come from doing everything right or fixing your life. It comes from the inside out, not the outside in.

WHEN WEIGHT BECOMES DYSREGULATION

Not everything that weighs us down is sin. Sometimes it's just . . . heavy. Hebrews 12:1 separates it for us: "Lay aside every weight, and the sin." Some things aren't sinful. They're just disruptive. Dysregulating.

So what does "dysregulation" even mean?

In clinical terms, emotional dysregulation is when we can't control our emotional responses or behaviors in ways that match the situation. Translation? You ever find yourself flipping out over something small? Or freezing up when you need to speak up? That's dysregulation. You're not broken—your system's overwhelmed.

Here's how it might show up:

Mood swings
Impulsiveness
Irritability
Trouble calming down after getting upset
Emotional or mental shutdown
Out-of-proportion reactions

Sound familiar? That's not just stress. That's your nervous system trying to scream, "I can't hold all of this!"

When I say I was gaming to find peace, what I was really doing was trying to regulate my nervous system. I was trying to get back to baseline, to feel something predictable in a world that felt chaotic.

And you know what? It worked. Temporarily. It gave me a sense of order, a feeling of control, even if it was all an illusion. For a little while it numbed the ache, quieted the grief, and gave me a reason to keep the lights on. But it didn't last. It couldn't. The peace it offered was synthetic—prepackaged calm in a world that was still storming. Sooner or later, it faded, and I was left holding a controller with no power to change what really hurt.

PEACE THAT REGULATES

Jesus said, "Peace I leave with you, My peace I give to you. . . . Let not your heart be troubled, neither let it be afraid" (John 14:27).

That peace isn't a cute phrase for bumper stickers. It's literal nervous-system regulation.

We don't talk about that enough in church. As a Pentecostal kid, I heard all about the Holy Spirit bringing power—healing, miracles, deliverance. But peace? That wasn't in the brochure.

But the truth is the Holy Spirit isn't just power for public ministry. He's peace for your private meltdown.

He regulates.

The gift of the Spirit isn't just tongues. It's groundedness. It's capacity. It's clarity. It's the ability to sit with your grief without being consumed by it. It's the ability to hold tension without falling apart.

This isn't overspiritualizing. It's integrative. It's the overlap between science and Spirit. Trauma dysregulates. The Spirit regulates. That's not metaphor—that's neurotheology.

When Jesus said, "Let not your heart be troubled," He was speaking therapy language. He was speaking trauma language. He was saying, "I see your nervous system. Let Me hold it with you." He was sitting your heart down on a couch across from His own, dropping a box of tissues into your lap, and telling you He's there to hold you while you let it all go.

He left us the Holy Spirit to give us literal peace—not a "there, there" pat on the head. He moves inside us to literally regulate our nervous systems.

God created these bodies we live in and abuse in various ways every day. He knows that we cannot be regulated when we are afraid. He knows that we cannot regulate if we are troubled. But it's when we lean in to the peace He gives us and regulate our nervous systems that we can be free—and not just from sin but from *any* maladaptive behavior.

Peace isn't pretending everything is fine. Peace is being able to admit everything isn't fine and still stay present. Peace is what I feel when I can scroll social media and not spiral. When I can disagree with someone without dissociating. When I can sit with a memory without my chest tightening like a vise.

And, by the way, "dissociation" is another trauma term that just means "I leave the moment because the moment feels too unsafe." Sometimes that's spacing out. Sometimes that's people-pleasing. Sometimes that's turning into a different version of yourself to survive the moment. All of that is a symptom of missing peace.

Therapy helped me name all of this. Let me pause here and say I'm not a therapist. I'm a man who goes to therapy. And if you need help, go get it. Don't pray instead of going to therapy. Pray and go to therapy.

My therapist helped me identify patterns, name dysregulation, and find tools to get back to peace. That doesn't mean therapy fixes everything, but it gave me language for what my spirit already knew.

MALADAPTIVE BEHAVIORS: THE BODY KEEPING THE SCORE

When you're dysregulated, your body will find a way to speak. What doesn't come up and out of your mouth through words will come up and out of your mouth through actions.

Maladaptive behaviors are coping strategies that work in the short term but hurt in the long term.[1] Think of them like duct tape on a leaky pipe. It might hold for a day. But it's not a fix.

Examples?

Porn and masturbation (this was my coping strategy)
Overwork
Binge eating or extreme diets
Isolation
Rage or passive-aggressive behavior

Chronic people-pleasing
Addictions (substances, screens, shopping)

All of these maladaptive behaviors come from the same root: pain that didn't get witnessed, so it mutated. But there's another way.

There is a peace that is accessible. There is a God who wants to regulate your system. There is a Spirit who lives inside you to guide you into wholeness. There are therapists, pastors, friends, safe spaces, and holy moments where you can breathe again.

You don't have to perform for that peace God offers. You don't have to prove yourself to God to get it. You don't have to hustle your way into wholeness. You just have to surrender. To stop patching up your wounds with distraction and let yourself be held.

Grab your coffee, your matcha, or whatever steady thing grounds you—but don't stop there. Grab your courage, your honesty, and your hope. You're about to step into sacred territory. We're not skimming the surface. We're going deep. Together. Let's go in—with hearts and eyes wide open for the peace we've been missing.

REFLECTION QUESTIONS

1. What have I been hunting for lately that I hoped would bring me peace?
2. How do I know when I'm dysregulated? What are my signs?
3. Have I noticed any maladaptive behaviors that are trying to speak for my pain?
4. Am I open to letting the Holy Spirit be a regulator, not just a rescuer?
5. What might it look like to experience peace in my nervous system?

2

SILENCE ISN'T GOLDEN

After more than twenty-six years of wrestling, unlearning, relearning, surrendering, and showing up, I finally feel like I live with peace. Not the Sunday-morning, shake-your-neighbor's-hand peace, but the kind that sits deep in my bones. The kind Jesus promised—the kind the Holy Spirit regulates. It's not perfection, and it didn't happen overnight. That timeline? It wasn't a typo. It took twenty-six and a half years.

Freedom doesn't happen in a flash. It unfolds like a slow sunrise. I used to wish it came on like a light switch. Clean. Immediate. Efficient. You hand your trauma to Jesus like a package at the post office and walk away with healing stamped and delivered. But that's not how it worked for me. It's not how it works for most of us. And let me say clearly: If your journey feels messy, unpredictable, or longer than you thought it would be, you aren't failing—you're healing.

When it came to Jesus, I brought all my pain with me, and the church, in all its sincerity, pointed me toward the altar. If you grew up in a Pentecostal church like I did, then you already know that the altar wasn't just a piece of furniture; it was the epicenter of everything. That's where it all went down. Demons got cast out. Hands were laid. People got wrecked under the power of the Holy Spirit. And listen, I'm not knocking any of that—I was shaped by those moments. Some of the deepest spiritual deposits in my life happened right there. I want to be crystal-clear on that, because I'm not trying to end up in hot water with the church mothers. If you know, you know.

But when it came to my trauma? The altar wasn't enough.

I remember being fresh in the faith bringing the full weight of my pain to the altar. I'd tell a person from the prayer team, "I was sexually abused when I was eight. I can't stop watching porn. I've had suicidal thoughts." And this person—whoever they were—simply wasn't ready. Their eyes got big. Their hands started shaking. "Lord," they prayed, "take this pain away." Then they started crying—because now they were triggered too. I had come looking for help, hoping to release what I'd been holding in. Instead, they were visibly unraveling right in front of me. So they prayed, I cried, the keys played softly in the background, and then I walked away—still carrying it all.

That's no shade to them. It's an indictment on how we treat trauma like a demon to cast out instead of a wound that needs tending. Because sometimes the most powerful spiritual experience isn't dramatic deliverance; it's patient care.

I need to be real clear here: Salvation is instant; healing is not. Getting saved? That's instant. Confess. Believe. Done. That's the beauty of grace. But healing? That's a process. It's not a microwave; it's a slow cooker. And sometimes it's an ICU.

For two years I went to every altar call hoping for freedom. Every single time I walked away thinking, *Maybe next time.* I saw other people testify, "God delivered me from this and that!" I was happy for them. But I wondered, *Why not me?*

Eventually I started believing that something was wrong with me. Like I had defective faith. Or a broken soul. I even started memorizing which altar workers prayed the best. "Who laid hands on you? I want to try that guy."

Then one day it clicked—it wasn't that I wasn't trying hard enough. It wasn't that my faith was broken or that I was spiritually defective. I had been doing everything I knew to do in church, and it still wasn't enough. What I needed wasn't just a moment at the altar. I needed a whole process. I needed therapy. I needed people who were more than anointed—I needed people who were trauma informed. People who understood how the brain and body hold pain, not just how to pray it away.

My soul didn't need more hype. My soul needed to cry out—and be heard, held, and helped.

I needed to break the silence.

MY SILENCE ALMOST KILLED ME

When Juliette and I started our first ministry in 1999, we called it Breaking the Silence Ministries based on Psalm 94:17. Because I knew silence had nearly buried me.

Here's the full story. I was sexually abused when I was eight years old by a neighbor who lived across the street—an older teenage boy. I didn't say a single word about it until I was nineteen. That's eleven years of silence. Eleven years of shame. Eleven years of pretending like everything was fine.

And it wasn't just me. Almost every other young boy on my block had been violated in the same way. We were all quiet, scared, ashamed, and confused. It felt like someone had put duct tape over my mouth. Only, after a while, it didn't feel like someone else was silencing me—it felt like I was the one putting the tape there. Every day. Over and over again. And when silence becomes your survival strategy, it starts to feel like your only option. Trauma taught me silence was safer than speaking. But trauma lies—and breaking the silence was how truth started to speak louder than the lies.

I was exposed to pornography when I was twelve years old. I remember the first image like it was burned into my brain. It felt like I drank that image into my soul. In that moment, I wasn't just seeing something—I was escaping something. That image made me feel something completely different from the trauma I had endured. It wasn't healing, but it was different—and different felt better. I was so relieved to feel *anything* other than the violation and confusion I had been carrying for years that I returned to that feeling over and over again.

Pornography and masturbation quickly became my comfort blanket, my secret retreat. It could've been alcohol, drugs, gambling, food—there are a hundred ways we try to numb our pain. Mine just happened to be porn and masturbation. I wasn't chasing pleasure as much as I was chasing numbness. I wanted to feel something else. I wanted to feel something different.

And I did. While porn did make me feel something other than the pain of my childhood trauma, it brought in massive amounts of shame and guilt. I didn't know how I'd ever break free from the grip it had on me. I can't tell you how many nights I felt tormented in my mind until I gave in to the temptations. I didn't know how I would ever stop. That's where my mom comes in.

When I was nineteen, my mom caught me watching porn. Imagine *that*. Two o'clock in the morning. Big-screen TV glowing like a spotlight in a dark room. Yeah—it was that long ago. This wasn't pocket porn. This wasn't high-speed internet on a cell phone or a hidden laptop behind closed doors. This wasn't even dial-up. This was VHS porn. Physical tape. Analog lust. You had to plan for it. Hide it. Rewind it. This was old-school.

And in that moment—caught red-handed—it should have been

the worst night of my life. The most humiliating. The kind of night you never forget for all the wrong reasons. But it wasn't.

It was actually the best night of my life. Because that was the night I finally had a chance to open my mouth and talk. To stop pretending. To stop hiding. To finally name the storm that had been raging in silence over eleven long years. I would never have prayed that my mom would catch me watching porn, but oftentimes getting caught is the most extravagant gift God can give us to break free of patterns that have overwhelmed our wills.

When I walked into my mom's room, she was on her knees praying. Not yelling. Not storming. Not shaming. She was praying. That image has stayed with me ever since—my mom, having just caught her son in what was most definitely his most shameful moment, on her knees interceding for me. That told me everything I needed to know. I wasn't reviled. I wasn't disgusting. I was still her son—and she was still praying for me.

I looked her in the eyes and finally let it out. I said, "Mom, I hope you don't think I'm a pervert. And I hope you don't think I'm nasty. But I was molested when I was eight years old."

That's exactly what I said. And those words came out cracked, trembling, and soaked in years of silence. But they were mine. That was the truth. That was the wound. And saying it out loud felt like breathing for the first time in eleven years. Like I had been holding my breath since I was a little boy, and finally—finally—I exhaled.

Then my younger brother admitted he'd been abused too. Then my dad, when he got home from the post office, told us he'd been abused as a child.

One confession opened the floodgates. One truth lit the path for more. And just like that we were no longer hiding in separate corners of the same house. We were broken together. And breaking together is better than bleeding alone.

One night. Three confessions. Four chains broken.

That living room turned into holy ground. Not because there

was incense burning or gospel music playing, but because truth broke the silence. And when truth breaks silence, healing starts breathing.

I need you to understand that God is not waiting for you to "clean up." He will take you in the middle of your mess. Minutes after watching porn and masturbating, through my confession, I was in the presence of the Lord. This will completely confuse your religious sensibilities, because we are taught to come as we are, until we actually do it, and then we come as *we are*. I hope you can read the difference in tone. I'm so grateful that God met my family that night in the middle of our pain and didn't wait for us to get back to church on Sunday. God didn't meet us in spite of our mess. He met us right in the thick of it, because His love isn't scared off by the reality of our struggle.

For years we were four people sitting at the same dinner table, each choking on our own invisible pain. And that night, a TV screen lit the room, but it was confession that lit our hearts. That's the night our family started healing. Not fully healed. But the bleeding stopped.

SOMEONE HAS TO GO FIRST

That's what I learned that night. Someone always has to go first. Confessing second is easy. Safe. Familiar. Confessing first? That takes guts. It takes grace. It takes the Holy Spirit breathing courage into your chest.

Going first means you're stepping out before you know who will catch you. Before you know whether anyone else will join you. It's like walking onto a stage with a spotlight in your eyes, trusting there's an audience out there even though you can't see them yet. But there's power in going first, because vulnerability isn't weakness—it's strength with skin on.

And when you go first, you make space for someone to go second. And third. And maybe even fourth. Because bravery is contagious. Courage doesn't echo in empty rooms—it multiplies in the hearts of those who hear it.

Therapy helped me name all of this. Again—let me be clear—I'm not a therapist. I'm a man who needed therapy and still does. If you need help, please go get it. Don't spiritualize it away. Don't pray your way around it when God might be nudging you to walk through it—with help.

We love to quote Psalm 23. The Lord is my Shepherd. Still waters. Green pastures. And that's real. But David also wrote Psalm 39. That one? Whole different vibe. "I was mute." "I did not open my mouth." "I am consumed." That's trauma language. That's the language of a man barely holding on.

David was a man of contrasts. He was anointed and flawed. Victorious and violated. Loved and despised. And what I love about him isn't that he always got it right. It's that he never faked it. David gave voice to pain, and he taught us that faith isn't about perfection—it's about honesty.

If you asked modern-day David how he was doing, he wouldn't hit you with "Blessed and highly favored." He'd say, "Honestly? I feel abandoned. I'm triggered. I'm praying but not sure anyone's listening. I'm exhausted. And I still believe that God is good."

That's the tension of trauma-informed faith. It holds both. It honors pain and clings to hope. It lets you sit in the valley *and* trust the Shepherd.

I grew up in a church culture that taught me to keep quiet. Don't embarrass us with your struggles; tell us how God made a way! Don't talk about that. Don't feel that. Don't need that. I knew those messages were unhelpful. I knew I was never going back to a life of silence.

Silence isn't golden when it costs you your peace.

Silence isn't sacred when it hides your suffering.

Silence isn't holy when it hinders your healing.

Speak. Cry. Text. Journal. Shout. Whisper. Groan. Whatever you do, don't stay silent. I don't care how it comes out—if it's through tears or voice notes or scribbles in a notebook. Just get it out. Naming it is how you loosen its grip. And healing doesn't require eloquence—it requires honesty.

When I told my mom, it wasn't a polished TED Talk. It was a messy, choked-up, stammering, shame-covered sentence. But it was mine. And it was real. And it was enough to crack open the door to freedom.

So if you're carrying something right now, I dare you—just open your mouth. Even a little. Let a whisper be the doorway to a roar.

Because this is the work. Not perfect speeches. Not pain-free paths. Just imperfect people like you and me and King David telling the truth and letting God do the rest. Healing isn't about getting it right—it's about getting it real.

REFLECTION QUESTIONS

1. What stories or secrets have I kept in silence?
2. Where did I learn that silence was safer than speaking?
3. What would it cost me to go first? What might it give someone else?
4. Who feels safe enough for me to be honest with?
5. What part of me has felt like it belonged in the grave?

3

CRY ME A RIVER

Sometimes what keeps me from reaching out—even when I know help is available—is grief. Not just sadness. I'm talking about the soul-heavy, breath-stealing, time-freezing kind of grief that sinks in deep and doesn't let go easily. Grief isn't just sadness—it's love with nowhere to go. It deserves space, compassion, and permission to move through us.

When my brother, Myles, died on September 17, 2004, there was no warning. No signs. No time to prepare. I talked to him the night before for forty-five minutes. The next morning, I woke up to a world that didn't have him in it. He was killed in a car accident and went to be with Jesus. Just like that.

Myles and I weren't twins, but we might as well have been. My mom dressed us like twins—same outfits, same shoes, same haircut. She'd send us into the fitting rooms like a matched set of mannequins. It wasn't because she didn't care what we liked. It was just easier. More efficient. Life was busy, and keeping us dressed alike was one less thing for her to juggle. I remember once telling her, "Mom, I like yellow." She just smiled and kept folding the matching blue shirts. She wasn't dismissive, just practical. That was her way.

We were twin adjacent—just seventeen months apart. I was born in June, and he came along in November of the following year. We were only one year apart in school, which meant we grew up in each other's pockets. This wasn't just my little brother—this was my first friend. My first best friend. My day one before I knew what day ones were. We learned how to live side by side—same cartoons, same chores, same love for basketball, same scraped knees from the same busted sidewalk out front. If you saw one of us, chances are the other one wasn't too far behind. That's how we rolled.

We weren't twins, but we shared a rhythm. Our lives were synced up. Even our friends knew it. When they called the house, nobody ever asked for just one of us. It was always "Can I speak to Tim *and* Myles?" That "and" mattered. That "and" was who we were.

So when he died, I didn't get closure. I didn't get that sacred walk down the corridor of death with him. No warning. No slow fade. No final moments to say, "I love you." No hand to hold while the breath left his body. Just a phone call that turned my world upside down.

It felt like the ground disappeared. Like I got dropped from a place I didn't know I'd climbed to. No safety net. No time to brace. Just free fall. I couldn't even scream. I just . . . fell. Traumatic loss like this doesn't just hurt emotionally; it shakes your sense of safety in the world. It's okay if that feels overwhelming or confusing; your nervous system is simply trying to make sense of the unimaginable.

I used to envy people who had time. I know that sounds wild, but it's true. I envied the families who sat by a hospital bed, as hard as that is. At least they got to say goodbye. At least they had the gift of preparing their hearts, even if it hurt. I got nothing. Just silence.

The kind that hums so loud it sounds like grief has a voice. The kind that fills the room and feels like it's pressing on your chest.

And that silence invited depression. It didn't announce itself; it just showed up. Took a seat like it lived there. And before I knew it, I wasn't just mourning—I was disappearing. Little by little, I felt like I was fading out of the life I used to know, and the only thing I could hear was that silence.

GRIEF HAS NO SCRIPT

I've always been an optimistic person. Joy comes naturally to me. I'm that "find the silver lining" kind of guy. But when Myles died, something in me split wide open. It wasn't sadness—it was a kind of grief so black and bottomless it swallowed everything that used to bring me life. Food had no taste. Light had no warmth. Even Juliette's touch, which had always been safe, felt foreign to me. I didn't want to be held. Didn't want to be seen. Didn't want light. Those were the darkest days I've ever known. Days when I couldn't tell where God stopped and the silence started. This wasn't spiritual weakness or a lack of faith; it was grief, and it needed acknowledgment, not correction.

And people—well-meaning, God-loving, Bible-quoting people—said the worst things.

Them: "Was he saved?"

Me: "Yes."

Them: "Then you'll see him again."

Me, in my mind: "*Whaaaaaaaaat?*"

I know they meant well, but that wasn't comfort. That was a shortcut around my pain. That's spiritual bypassing. That's putting a Band-Aid on a bullet wound.

One person looked me straight in the eye and said, "I believe you're going to have a greater anointing now."

I could've screamed. I didn't want a greater anointing. I wanted my brother.

So I did what broken people do—I pulled in. I wrapped my grief around me like a weighted blanket laced with thorns. I held it close. Let it fester. Let it grow roots in my chest. And somewhere in that fog I told God I was done. Done preaching. Done pretending. Done with Him.

But even in my tantrum, He stayed.

Even in my silence. Even in my bitterness. Even when my fists were clenched in anger and my lips refused to pray—He stayed.

It was like trying to hold grief in one hand and God in the other, and they both felt too heavy. I didn't know how to carry both. I thought I had to choose. I thought grief disqualified me from closeness with God.

But He never left. He didn't lecture me. Didn't correct me. Didn't hit me with a verse. He just sat there. In the dark. With me. God isn't just comfortable with our grief; He meets us precisely where grief has led us, without demanding immediate healing or hurried hope.

And that's when I learned something sacred: God is the best kind of therapist—because He knows when to speak, and He knows when to just sit in silence beside you until you're ready to breathe again.

One of my therapists, Nancy Houston, used to say, "Tim, you need to do your grief work." I didn't want to hear it. At first, I didn't.

Grief work means intentionally sitting with your pain. It means moving through the five stages—denial, anger, bargaining, depression, acceptance—knowing they aren't linear. You might loop around. You might stall. You might regress. It's not a checklist. It's a cycle. And it's okay if your cycle looks different from everyone else's—grief has no script or timeline.

I didn't do the work right away. I eventually did—but looking back, I wish I had started sooner. If I could go back and talk to myself in those early days, I'd say, "Don't wait." Because the healing didn't come from pushing grief away. It came from facing it head-on. And the sooner you face it, the sooner peace can start to find you.

MAKING PEACE WITH GRIEF

In January 2024 my father, Charles Edward Ross, was diagnosed with bile duct cancer. Ever heard of it? We hadn't either. It blindsided us. For the record, I completely and utterly hate cancer.

Quick breakdown: The bile duct connects your liver, gallbladder, and small intestine. It helps your body digest food.[1] When cancer hits that system, it spreads fast. It's rare. It's aggressive. Only about twenty thousand cases a year. And the five-year survival rate? Just over 21 percent.[2]

We didn't have five years. We didn't even have one. From the moment he was admitted to the hospital to the day he passed, it was only seven weeks. The last stretch, he was at home in hospice care. And when the time came, he passed peacefully. February 24, 2024.

This man—my hero—was gone.

And three days later, February 27, my book *Welcome to the Basement* was released. Two days after that, February 29, I went on a monthlong book tour. So in five days I went from saying goodbye to my daddy to boarding a flight.

The schedule was locked. Flights booked. Events announced. No time to reschedule. No space to unravel. And I was stuck wondering, *Am I running from my grief?* Sometimes grief is quiet, waiting for you to pause long enough to feel it. It's wise to periodically check in with yourself, or with someone who knows you deeply, to ensure grief isn't silently steering your decisions.

I didn't know, so I asked Juliette. I asked my boys. I asked my mom. I couldn't trust my own instincts in that moment.

And they helped me land on something that freed me: They reminded me that I don't hide my feelings. I can bring them with me. Grief isn't something we can outrun—it's something we learn to walk beside, acknowledging its presence without letting it define our entire journey.

If I was going to do this tour, my grief was going to tour with me.

So that's what I did. I made peace with my grief.

I've learned not to suppress it. Not to ignore it. When grief shows up, I schedule a meeting with it. I give it room to speak. I don't let it drive, but I don't lock it in the trunk either.

Grief demands our attention. If we ignore it, it doesn't disappear. It multiplies. It will sneak into the next season and sabotage everything you care about.

That's why I cry when I need to. That's why I walk with my grief instead of away from it.

I also learned something else in those dark moments: God is not fragile.

He doesn't flinch when we fall apart. He doesn't shut down when we raise our voice. He doesn't walk away when we break down. He holds us—right there in the mess. God's strength isn't revealed by shielding Himself from our pain; it's revealed by how gently He holds our broken pieces until we're ready to pick them up again.

God isn't petty. He doesn't keep receipts. He's not scrolling through your past like He's trying to build a case against you. He's not shocked by your tears or offended by your anger.

He sees me as His child. Not in a "sit down and be quiet" kind of way, but in a "you're safe to feel this" kind of way.

Some of us didn't grow up with that kind of safety. Some of us had parents who couldn't handle our feelings. "Don't talk to me like that." "Who do you think you are?" "You better fix your face."

We learned early: *Feelings are dangerous*. Anger was disrespect. Sadness was weakness. So what do we do now? We walk on eggshells with God. We edit our prayers. We try to sound healed when we're still bleeding. But hear me: God is not your earthly dad. God is not your earthly mom. God is not the father who left. He's not the mother who made you feel like too much. He's not Odin, Zeus, or Thor. He's not some mythical being waiting to strike you down with lightning because you're not "spiritual" enough.

God is a good Father. A safe Father. The kind of Father who sits with you in the dark and doesn't say a word until you're ready to hear it.

He won't punish your honesty with silence. He won't betray your trust. He'll sit with you—until the shaking stops, until the tears dry, until you're strong enough to get up again.

Some of y'all need to cry.

I'm not talking about misty eyes and dabbing corners. I'm talking about a full-body, shoulder-shaking, can't-catch-your-breath cry. Yes, the ugly cry. Because if you don't? The next season will pay for the last one you didn't mourn. And if you're wondering whether God can handle it, let me tell you: He already has.

TEARS ARE CONNECTION

I used to walk six miles most days at a park down the street from my house. One morning I passed a young woman who was crying—full-on, couldn't-hide-it crying.

She wiped her face, said, "Good morning," and kept walking.

I took out my earbuds and asked, "Are you okay?"

She nodded and whispered, "Yeah, I'm okay."

I didn't try to fix her. I asked so she'd know someone saw her. So she'd know it was okay to cry. Her vulnerability pulled me in. It made me care.

There's something powerful about tears.

Science backs this up. Studies show that crying triggers

comfort—not just for the one crying, but for those witnessing it. It's a bonding tool. Crying communicates need, and we are wired to respond to that.[3]

Our tears are thicker when we cry from emotion versus when we cry from chopping onions.[4] They carry stress hormones and release tension. They're literal vehicles for healing.

Your tears are sacred.

We think we have to hold it together. We think strength is silence. We think we're protecting others by hiding our pain.

We're not. We're robbing them of connection.

Tears build bridges. They create space for empathy. They invite others in. So cry. Cry when it hurts. Cry when you're confused. Cry when you remember. Cry when you miss someone. Cry when the moment is too big. Cry when it's too loud. Cry when it's too quiet.

Your tears don't scare God. They don't scare me. They're part of what makes you human. So cry. And let the river run. Every tear you shed is holy ground. Your vulnerability isn't a burden—it's an offering of trust, courage, and authenticity.

REFLECTION QUESTIONS

1. When was the last time I allowed myself to really cry?
2. Am I carrying grief I've never acknowledged?
3. Who have I lost that I haven't mourned?
4. What have I been pretending doesn't hurt?
5. What would it look like to let my tears be seen?

4

A FIRE OF WORDS

Have I ever been so angry that the more I thought about it, the more the fire grew inside me? Absolutely. I've been there. That kind of anger doesn't just hit your heart—it hits your nervous system like a grenade. Anger isn't inherently bad; it's a signal from your nervous system that something important to you feels threatened or violated. The key isn't suppression; it's careful expression.

I'll paint a scene you might recognize.

You're leaving work. There's that coworker—the one who manages to get under your skin with nothing more than the way they breathe during meetings. You had a disagreement earlier in the day. It seemed small at the time. You brushed it off. Walked away. Said to yourself, *That was weird. I'm good.*

But then you're driving home. The radio's playing, but in your head you're replaying the whole thing. Again and again.

I can't believe they said that.

I should've said . . .

Who do they think they are?

And the more you think, the hotter you get. By the time you hit your driveway, you're not walking in the door, you're walking into a war zone of unprocessed emotion. Someone asks how you are. You say, "Fine." But everything in you is screaming.

The pot is boiling. And all it takes is someone forgetting to pass you the hot sauce at dinner, and suddenly you're yelling. Loud. Intense. All that pent-up fury comes pouring out on someone who doesn't even deserve it.

I remember reading Psalm 39:3 and thinking, *David gets it.* "My heart was hot within me; while I was musing, the fire burned. Then I spoke with my tongue."

Translation: The more I sat with it, the more it cooked inside me. Then I exploded.

REPRESSED ANGER IS STILL FIRE

I've learned something in therapy that changed how I process moments like that: When I don't give my anger a voice, it finds its own volume. That volume doesn't always come out in words. Sometimes it comes out in sarcasm. Sometimes in avoidance. Sometimes in rage. It leaks. It erupts. It hijacks moments. Unaddressed anger doesn't disappear—it waits beneath the surface, often disguising itself as anxiety, bitterness, or even physical pain. Naming anger directly is how we keep it from controlling us indirectly.

I experienced this firsthand in group therapy. (More on that later, but imagine a circle of folks committed to healing, all doing the work of naming their pain together.)

There was a spiritual wound I'd never voiced. Deep, unresolved. I'd never confronted the person who hurt me. Never had the chance. And my therapist—brilliant and trauma informed—told me something wild: You don't need the person in the room to heal the wound. Your body just needs the truth.

So we role-played.

She said, "Pick someone in the group to play the person who wounded you. Sit across from them and say what you need to say."

The man I picked pulled up a chair. I sat across from him.

Now, I was the only Black man in that room. That is important to note because the way I needed to express myself in that moment was about to catch my White homies off guard. As the conversation started, so did the fire.

I began calm. Thoughtful. Controlled.

Then my voice started rising.

Then I was shouting.

Then I was screaming.

Every expletive. Every emotion. Every ounce of heartbreak I'd stuffed down over the years erupted. That room became my battleground, my sanctuary, my courtroom, my confessional. It was street-level honesty. Raw. Unfiltered.

And when it was over? I felt light. Like something had been lifted off my chest that I didn't even realize I'd been carrying for decades. My body—my actual body—felt freer. Because it had finally spoken.

Here's what I've learned: Feelings can't just stay feelings. Our brains need words to heal. Language brings structure. Language brings order. When we take what's swirling in our soul and give it oratorical form, when we put words to what's been buried, our nervous system responds. The body exhales. The heart slows. The mind finds clarity. My body didn't just react; it found relief. It regulated. It released.

The moment was intense. No one in that group had ever seen me like that. But they didn't run. They didn't recoil. They gave me an extravagant gift—containment. They held space for my rage, my pain, my truth.

And in that space I experienced something that changed my life: full closure.

I didn't have to speak to the person who hurt me. But I spoke the truth anyway. And that was enough. That was healing. That was the fire finally burning out—without burning me down.

The man across from me was shook. But he didn't move. He stayed present. And in doing that, he showed me something I'll never forget: People who truly love you can handle all of you. When anger is given safe, structured expression—like in a therapeutic environment or trusted relationship—it can move from being a destructive force to becoming a powerful gateway to clarity and healing.

There's a clinical model called trauma-informed stabilization treatment, or TIST, developed by trauma specialist Janina Fisher.[1] One of its core beliefs is that parts of us hold trauma and need a voice, not exile. That our healing depends not on ignoring the wounded part but on welcoming it with compassion and clarity. Naming pain isn't a sign of weakness—it's an act of bravery and compassion toward ourselves. Our wounded parts don't heal through silence; they heal through being seen, heard, and validated.

That's what I experienced that day in group.

I didn't need that person to apologize. I needed my body to feel like it was finally safe enough to say, "That hurt." And when I did, my parts—those younger, hurt versions of me—finally exhaled.

You might be thinking, *Tim, if I showed up with my full truth, my people wouldn't know what to do with me.* And I get that. I've felt that too.

Here's the thing: Each of us—every human being—longs for five things:

1. To be fully seen
2. To be fully heard
3. To be fully known

4. To be fully loved
5. To be fully agreed with

Did you notice that last one? Yeah, we're not guaranteed agreement. Those first four, though? Every human on earth needs those first four, and four out of five ain't bad.

Even God is four out of five. He sees us. Hears us. Knows us. Loves us. But agrees with us? Not always.

And yet the relationship still holds.

So if you've got someone in your life who gives you four out of five? Cherish that. That's more than most people get. Agreement isn't a prerequisite for intimacy. Being seen, heard, known, and loved is. Your fullness isn't a flaw—it's your authenticity. And authentic relationships can hold tension without breaking under the weight of honesty.

DON'T LOSE YOUR FLAVOR

When I launched my podcast, I was still code-switching.

Let me be real—I wasn't trying to sound "pastoral" in the traditional churchy sense. It was more like I was using my "State of the Union" voice—the version of me that felt formal, polished, and appropriate for public consumption. You know the difference. It's like when a president is speaking at a press conference versus when he's just talking with folks on the golf course or at a private dinner. There are different voices for different settings. And for years I thought ministry required me to stay in that formal voice. But when I launched the podcast, I realized I didn't have to stay in that space anymore. I could talk the way I talk. Be the way I am. All of me could finally show up.

Until that moment I held back pieces of myself. I wasn't lying—I was just performing a version of me I thought people needed. I trimmed my voice. Tucked in my edges. Smoothed out my slang. Not because I was ashamed of who I was but because I'd been trained to think certain rooms could handle only a certain kind of presence.

But in doing that, I lost something real. Not my salvation. Not my calling. But my *flavor.* God never called us to lose our distinction to fit a mold. He called us knowing exactly who we were—every nuance, every quirk, every cultural context—and He uses all of it, masterfully.

I was made to show up in this world in a God-flavored, LA-seasoned, Inglewood-born way. But I forgot in spite of where I came from; He called me *because* of it.

And then 2020 hit. And the world flipped.

Racial tensions boiled. White folks started asking questions. Reading books. Listening to stories from Black folks they'd never stopped to hear before. For the first time it felt like some people genuinely wanted to understand—not fix, not debate—just understand.

And in that moment I felt the tension: Would I keep code-switching to keep them comfortable? Or would I finally let all of me show up?

I remembered who I was. I'm all things Cali. All things Inglewood. I absorbed hip-hop culture, gang culture, Jesus culture—and, somehow, God braided that all together to reach a generation that wouldn't trust anything less than real.

I know my identity in Christ comes first. Absolutely. But my ethnicity? My Blackness? That's the flavor. That's the texture. That's the lens through which I've experienced grace, grief, and growth. God saved me and changed me, but He didn't erase me. He saved me and partners with me—as I am. Because it takes all of me to reach the people I'm called to right now. I was made for this dispensation. This moment in time. This generation. They're wide open!

And the moment I stopped managing people's perceptions, the most authentic people showed up.

Now? I show up as all of me.

If someone comes up and says, "Tim, I've been listening for three years. I love the show," I know they've heard it all. The raw. The vulnerable. The theological. The hood. The Spirit-filled.

And they stayed.

But what about the people who don't stay? Here's my word to you: Let them go. If they can't handle your grief, your process, your past, your truth—let them walk.

Let them go if your history triggers them. Let them go if your honesty intimidates them. Let them go if your healing is incompatible with their image of you.

And listen—this isn't arrogance. This isn't coldness. This is clarity. This is self-differentiation.

Self-differentiation means knowing who you are and where you end. It's the ability to stay rooted in your identity—even when others want to pull you into roles you've outgrown or images you never chose. It's not rebellion. It's maturity. It's the steady, Spirit-led courage to say, "I'm still me, even if you don't understand me anymore."

Letting people go doesn't mean you don't love them. It means you refuse to lose yourself to keep them.

You were never meant to perform your way into being loved. You were never created to babysit other people's comfort zones. You are not too much. You are not too complicated. You are not too real. You are just enough—for the right people. Self-differentiation isn't selfishness—it's stewardship. It's honoring who God made you to be, even when others don't fully understand.

I've said it before, and I'll say it again—David was a gangster of honesty. This man went from writing Psalm 23 to Psalm 88 like he was dropping mixtapes from different emotional zip codes. One moment he was lying down in green pastures. The next? He was saying, "Darkness is my closest friend" (Ps. 88:18 NLT). And God still called him "a man after His own heart" (1 Sam. 13:14). Not because he always got it right. Not because he never sinned. But because he told the truth.

David showed us that intimacy with God is built not by perfect behavior but by honest conversations—even messy ones.

LIVING IN SILENCE ISN'T NOBLE. IT'S HARMFUL.

When I live in silence, I live in secrets. And secrets rot the soul. Not metaphorically—literally. They fester in the body. They hijack the nervous system. They sabotage relationships, because what we don't speak, we end up leaking.

There is no prize for pretending. No trophy for keeping it together while you fall apart inside. You don't get extra credit in the kingdom for being a vault. You don't become holy by becoming invisible.

Some of us were taught that strength means silence. That loyalty means keeping secrets. That maturity means swallowing pain. But real strength is in confession. Real growth is in naming what hurt. Real healing is in releasing what's been locked up.

Your soul doesn't need more discipline. Your soul needs more space. Space to feel. Space to cry. Space to scream if it needs to. Space to say, "This is what happened," and not feel ashamed.

So speak. Cry. Write. Shout. Whisper. Whether it's to a therapist, a journal, a friend, or God Himself—give your soul words. Because words are the doorways to freedom. Breaking silence isn't betrayal; it's liberation. When we speak our truth, we break the chains that shame uses to hold us hostage. You were not designed to carry this alone. And there is someone out there worthy of walking with you through it all.

Don't wait until you explode. Don't wait until the body keeps the score. Tell the truth now—before your silence costs you everything.

REFLECTION QUESTIONS

1. Who is safe enough to hear my truth?
2. Have I been holding anger that needs expression?
3. What parts of me have been silenced?
4. What would it feel like to be fully seen, heard, and loved?
5. Am I willing to let people go who love only a filtered version of me?

5

VULNERABILITY IS A SUPERPOWER

Even when I know how important it is to break the silence—to give my soul words—there are still moments when vulnerability feels terrifying. There's risk involved in being open. Sharing what's real can expose old wounds, shake relationships, and leave me wondering who I can trust.

There have been seasons when I wanted to open up to a believer, but I couldn't stomach the idea of being hit with a Bible verse I already knew or a reminder to "just trust God." It wasn't that I didn't trust Him. I did. I still do. It was just that life was punching me in the face at the time. Rent was due. Gas was up. Groceries weren't cheap. And my salary? Just enough to survive, not enough to breathe.

And then there were the times I thought about going to a friend who wasn't a believer. Someone I grew up with. Someone I knew would keep it real. Someone familiar—homegrown. But I held back. Not because I thought they'd throw it in my face but because I wasn't sure they knew how to hold the tension. The tension of seeing me struggle and still believing my faith was real. The tension of hearing my pain without using it as evidence that God had failed me. I didn't want to become another example of why they walked away from the church.

So I found myself caught between two doors, both of them risky. I wanted to talk to someone—I needed to—but I couldn't figure out who could hold my pain without misusing it.

Maybe you've been there. Maybe you finally opened up to someone. Told a friend about your struggles. Only to walk away from that conversation feeling worse. Maybe they broke your trust. Or tried fixing you instead of listening to you. Or acted weird around you afterward, like your truth made them uncomfortable.

I see your fear. I get it. Vulnerability is risky.

It means letting someone into the messy parts of your soul. The unfiltered pain. The confusion. The stuff that doesn't have a bow on it yet. And yes—there's always the chance they could misuse that access. And when they do? It leaves a bruise. Sometimes a scar. When someone misuses your vulnerability, it's painful—but it doesn't diminish your worth or the value of your story. The misuse reflects the other person's capacity, not your character.

I've been there. I've put myself out there before—publicly and privately—and I've been betrayed. I've felt the sting of opening up only to be mishandled, misread, or misunderstood. And after that happens, something inside says, "Never again."

But here's the thing: That voice is trying to protect you, not heal you. And protection without healing leads to isolation.

Vulnerability is kind of my default setting now—but it didn't start that way. It's a practice I chose and keep choosing, even after pain. Because I've learned that while some people can't hold what I carry, others can—and do. The risk is still real. But the reward is life-changing.

So if you've been hurt by vulnerability gone wrong, I see you. I validate that pain. But don't let one experience—or even a few—become your blueprint for every future connection. Healing involves recognizing when hurtful experiences become limiting beliefs, and intentionally rewriting those narratives with healthier truths.

That's why the next part matters so much: Not everyone deserves access.

NOT EVERYONE DESERVES ACCESS

Here's a truth I've learned: Just because one person betrayed your vulnerability doesn't mean everyone will. Not everyone is Janet. Not everyone is Thomas. (Some random Janet and Thomas just caught strays.) Yes, they hurt you. That happened. And it wasn't okay.

But you can't give one person's failure permission to shape the rest of your life.

Listen: Don't globalize the pain. Janet might've dropped the ball. Thomas might've fumbled your trust. But they're not everybody. You haven't met everybody. You had a real experience, but if you turn that experience into a belief about the entire world, that belief will start to limit your life. And that's not protection—that's imprisonment.

All men aren't dogs. All women aren't gold diggers. All leaders aren't narcissists. All churches aren't toxic. Yes, someone burned you. Yes, they mishandled your heart. But if you stay stuck in that betrayal, you're going to miss the people who were actually built to hold you well.

So be wise. Be slow. Don't hand out the keys to everyone. Not everyone deserves access. But don't let cynicism become your compass. Pain will lie to you if you let it drive. Discernment in relationships is wisdom—but building walls out of fear prevents both hurt and healing. The key is learning to build gates, not walls—opening selectively, but not sealing off entirely.

There's still good out there. There are still safe people. And you still deserve to be known.

TRY A THERAPIST

One of the safest places I've ever told the truth about myself was in therapy.

Therapists are legally bound to confidentiality. That means they can't gossip about your story or weaponize your weakness. And if you find a therapist you don't click with? You can switch. No drama. No explanation required.

I'm not a licensed clinician, but therapy has been a sacred part of my healing journey. It gave me language for things I didn't know how to name. It helped me understand what was happening in my brain, my body, and my spirit.

And I'll be honest—the first time I went, I was desperate. There wasn't anything polished or noble about it. I was drowning. I needed help. And sitting with someone who didn't flinch at my truth? That was holy ground. Therapy isn't admitting defeat—it's a courageous act of stewardship, acknowledging your soul deserves safe professional care.

The very first therapist I went to, I told everything: the abuse, the porn addiction, the shame, the suicidal thoughts. I waited for him to look shocked, disgusted, offended.

He didn't.

He just nodded and said, "That makes sense. Based on what you've been through, that's a very understandable response."

Wait . . . what?

He repeated it: "You're not crazy. You're surviving. And we can help you heal."

No judgment. No Scripture shaming. And this was a Christian therapist. He didn't whip out a Bible verse. He didn't rebuke me. He held space. He listened.

That day, I realized something else too: God is a therapist.

The first therapy question God asked in the Bible is in Genesis 3:9: "Where are you?"

He wasn't asking Adam for GPS coordinates. He's omniscient. He's omnipresent. He knew exactly where Adam was. That question was for Adam.

That was God saying, "Let's locate you. Not your body. Your soul. Your state of mind."

And when Adam tried to deflect with "I was afraid because I was naked; and I hid" (Gen. 3:10), God followed up with another question: "Who told you that?" (v. 11).

God wasn't being rhetorical. He was peeling back the layers. That's therapy. That's the Spirit at work, gently guiding us to truth. And let's be clear—these aren't just divine icebreakers. These are clinical questions. Any trauma-informed therapist will tell you healing begins with locating the self and identifying the voices that shaped your story. That's foundational work.

What God did with Adam mirrors the clinical approach to trauma recovery. A good therapist doesn't just address what you did—they help you understand why. They slow down the story. They trace the fear. They help you name the lie. That's what God was doing.

"Where are you?" is a grounding question. "Who told you that?" is a cognitive-reframing question. God was doing therapeutic work before therapy had a name. Understanding that God's questions invite self-awareness rather than shame can transform our prayers from scripted monologues into authentic dialogues of healing.

So yes—God is a healer. God is a redeemer. And God, in the most sacred way, is also a therapist.

UNSPOKEN PAIN BECOMES BITTERNESS

Psalm 39:2 says, "I was mute with silence, I held my peace even from good; and my sorrow was stirred up." When I stop talking about the bad, I slowly stop talking about the good too. And what's left is bitterness. Cynicism. Numbness.

Think about it: When someone gives you five compliments and one critique, what do you obsess over? Exactly.

Our brains are wired for survival, and negativity sticks. That's why unspoken pain festers. Bitterness isn't a character flaw—it's unprocessed pain. And unprocessed pain can make us feel stuck in the negative.

I've seen it in real life:

You share good news—"I got a promotion!"—and someone replies, "That's great, but now you'll have more stress. Hope the raise was worth it."

You announce your engagement, and someone says, "You know 50 percent of marriages end in divorce, right?"

You're trying to enjoy Thanksgiving when a relative says, "What do we even have to be thankful for? This world is falling apart."

That's what happens when people never deal with the pain they refuse to talk about. They stop celebrating. They can't see the light anymore.

But when we put words to that hurt, it breaks the cycle of internalized negativity, creating space for genuine joy to return.

Imagine a community where someone could say, "I'm not okay today. God is good, but I'm not." And the response wasn't correction or a spiritual lecture but compassion. "Thank you for sharing that. I'll be praying for you. Anything specific I can pray for?"

"Yeah, I lost my job. It's been hard providing for my family."

"I can identify with what you're going through. I'm here." That's it. No fixing. No forcing. No fake smiles. Just presence. That's what I dream about. That's what I'm trying to live.

I believe that God is calling us to build a new kind of church. A new culture within His church where emotional honesty is spiritual maturity. Where faith isn't measured by how well you hide your pain but by how safely you bring it to the light.

What would it look like to preach sermons that calibrate people to both the pleasures and the pains of life? What if we reminded people that God is not only present on our best days but especially on our worst? That Jesus Himself said that "in this life we will have trouble," and He meant it (John 16:33). That the heroes of the faith in Hebrews 11 weren't all parting seas and shutting lions' mouths—some were sawed in two, wandered in deserts, and never received the promises of God in this lifetime.

And yet God called them faithful.

Both kinds of stories were included. Both were commended. Because faith isn't just about the outcome—it's about the offering. A healthy church culture doesn't demand perpetual positivity. It makes room for lament, recognizing that honest expression of sorrow deepens our worship rather than diminishes it.

That's the culture I'm believing God for.

A place where you don't have to smile to belong. Where tears are allowed to fall. Where we can normalize the full human experience in the presence of a holy God.

Sometimes the holiest thing I can do is feel the ugly, let the tears fall, and then walk forward in honesty.

Because vulnerability isn't weakness.

It's sacred.

It's courageous.

It's a superpower.

REFLECTION QUESTIONS

1. What haven't I talked about yet?
2. What am I currently suppressing that needs to be grieved?
3. Is my inner child with me in the present, or am I stuck in the past with my inner child?
4. What would it look like to feel safe enough to tell the truth?

6

TURN ON THE LIGHTS

My journey with therapy has stretched nearly thirty years. That's not a typo. Before terms like "mental health," "self-care," "triggered," and "narcissist" were TikTok sound bites, I was sitting on someone's chair or couch getting it in. That's almost thirty years of sitting in rooms, talking through wounds, naming what hurt, and learning to see myself honestly. Not for my image. Not even just for my family. For me.

I knew I didn't like where I was mentally and emotionally. I didn't want to stay in that place. And I was willing to do the work.

If you're starting to feel that same tug, let me say this up front: Trauma evolves with time, and therapy isn't a one-time fix. It's not a spiritual car wash. It's a process. It's maintenance. And sometimes it's triage.

One of the hardest truths about trauma is that it shape-shifts. A car accident might make it hard to get behind the wheel the next day. A year later you're driving again, but the sound of tires screeching on the freeway brings it all back. Suddenly you're gripped with anxiety, unsure why your body is reacting like the accident happened just yesterday.

That's how trauma works. It lives in the body, and it resurfaces in layers—sometimes in new seasons, sometimes in old triggers dressed in new clothes.

The same goes for childhood trauma, spiritual abuse, relational betrayal. You might have "gotten over it" in one way, but as you evolve, the pain finds new angles. New questions. New grief.

Therapy has helped me revisit the same stories again and again, each time uncovering something I wasn't ready to see before. It's not regression. It's revelation. Revisiting trauma is an act of courage and self-awareness, allowing deeper layers of healing to take place each time.

And in the process I've also learned that healing isn't about dumping feelings. It's about confession.

Now, I know that word comes loaded depending on your background. Maybe you grew up associating confession with guilt and shame. Or maybe it feels performative, like something you say to check a religious box.

Let me redefine it. Confession is not just about admission. It's about acknowledgment.

Admission says, "I did it." Acknowledgment says, "I did it, and I see what it cost me. I want to change."

That's what Scripture means when it talks about confession. First John 1:9 says that "if we confess our sins, He is faithful and just to forgive." But it doesn't stop there. It says walking in the light leads to fellowship (v. 7). That hit me differently the more I sat with it. Confession isn't punishment. It's connection. It's restoration. It's reconnection.

Confession shifts us from isolated shame into the safety of relational intimacy—where healing thrives.

Confession is the start of salvation. Romans 10:9 says, "If you confess with your mouth the Lord Jesus and believe in your heart that God has raised Him from the dead, you will be saved." That's not a footnote—that's foundational. That's the entry point into the kingdom.

And it's not just about eternity. It's about emotional and spiritual oxygen in the here and now. I remember when I confessed to my mom that I had been abused—I was nineteen years old. That confession felt like two thousand pounds of concrete came off my chest. The weight didn't lift because the circumstances changed. It lifted because I stopped carrying it alone. Carrying shame alone convinces us we're uniquely broken, but confession reveals that we're profoundly human and deeply worthy of grace. That's the power of confession. Not because it magically erases pain but because it moves the pain from secrecy into light. And whatever lives in the light loses its grip in the dark.

If we want peace, we need truth. And if we want truth, we have to confess. Not just to God but to ourselves. To people we trust. To the parts of our souls that stopped believing we were worth healing. Confession isn't just a holy act. It's a healing one.

ALIGNING WITH THE TRUTH

When I got saved in 1996, I was a born-again porn addict. Some religious folks choke on that statement. As though the blood of Jesus should've instantly deleted my browser history and rewired my brain overnight.

It didn't.

My spirit was made new, yes. But my soul had some miles to go.

Porn had rewired my brain. It trained me to chase a dopamine high with the click of a button. It created neurological pathways that linked stress, boredom, anxiety, or even celebration to self-soothing through arousal. And that wiring didn't disappear just because I got baptized.

But let's zoom out.

Because this isn't just about porn. This is about addiction. All of it. Whether it's the scroll of Instagram, the thrill of a shopping spree, the rush of validation, the escape of gaming, the "just one more episode" loop of Netflix, or the sugar hit from another doughnut—your brain gets the same dopamine fix. So before you disqualify yourself from this part of the story, pause.

You might not be addicted to porn. But you're probably getting the same chemical payoff from something else. Your wax just comes in a different wrapper.

Addiction isn't about weakness—it's about wiring. And unlearning that wiring takes time. It took me years. And I mean years. Not because God isn't powerful but because healing often comes through process, not lightning bolt.

I had to walk out my healing. I had to confess. Not just to God but to mentors, counselors, and friends. I had to stop hiding behind spiritual language and admit what was going on inside me.

And I had to acknowledge it too. No matter how much I felt drawn to pornography and masturbation, I had to come into agreement with what God said about it. Not just that it was sin but that it was costing me intimacy, peace, clarity, and self-worth.

If it were up to me, I might still be indulging in it. But Jesus isn't just my Savior—He's my Lord. That means I don't just ask Him to rescue me. I surrender to Him to lead me.

That's confession. That's agreement. That's turning on the light. Confession brings our struggles into alignment with God's truth about our inherent worth and dignity.

VERTICAL AND HORIZONTAL CONFESSION

Confession is twofold. There's vertical confession—me and God. And there's horizontal confession—me and others. And both are vital, but they're not the same.

Let's be real. Vertical confession does something that horizontal confession never can. And horizontal confession does something vertical confession doesn't touch.

Here's the breakdown: When I confess to God—1 John 1:9–style—I receive cleansing. Not partial. Not performative. Full, soul-deep cleansing. That kind of restoration doesn't come from another person. No man can cleanse you. That's God's lane, and He made that possible through the finished work of Jesus on the cross.

But if you stop there, you miss something major. Because Jacob 5:16 (or, as most like to call it, James 5:16) says, "Confess your faults one to another, and pray one for another, that ye may be healed" (KJV).

So track with me: God cleanses. People help us heal. Cleansing is vertical. Healing is horizontal.

There is an order to this. God comes first. Always. Because if I'm not honest with Him, I'm not going to be honest with anyone else. I might *say* the right things, but it'll be performative. A mask. A well-crafted monologue with no weight.

But when I get real with God first, then choose to be vulnerable with people who are safe? Healing hits different. Restoration has layers, and it begins with honesty, both heavenward and humanward.

That's the power of confession. Cleansing from God. Healing with people. Both sacred. Both necessary. Vertical confession restores intimacy with God; horizontal confession restores intimacy with community. Both are essential because healing thrives not just in divine connection but in human connection as well.

REVEAL AND HEAL

Have you ever tried walking through your house in the dark?

You know the layout. You're confident. You think, *I don't need the light. I've got this.*

Until you stub your toe on the coffee table. Or step on a Lego. Or hip-check the bathroom door.

That's what it's like living with hidden pain. You know your life. You think you can manage. But sooner or later something hidden in the dark takes you out.

And let me just say it plain—like my folks from Birmingham and East Texas used to say—"Keep doing it if you want to." That's country talk for "It's your choice, but it won't end well." It's the warning wrapped in wisdom. "Keep running around that pool if you want to. You about to bust your head wide open."

You think you can handle that darkness without turning on the light? Okay. Keep it to yourself if you want to. But don't act surprised when you find yourself tripping over the same emotional coffee table again and again. That's what happens when you try to navigate pain without confession. You keep bumping into stuff you won't admit is even there.

Confession turns on the lights. Living without confession is like navigating an emotional minefield blindfolded. Turning on the lights isn't just wise—it's compassionate self-care. It doesn't always fix the mess, but it shows you what you're dealing with. And once you can see it, you can start to heal it.

Now, some folks twist grace into a pass to avoid confession altogether. "I'm already forgiven, so why confess?"

Because confession isn't for God's benefit. It's for yours.

God already knows. He saw it before you did. He's not shocked. Psalm 139 says He knows your thoughts from afar. Before you were formed in your mother's womb, He knew you. If you ascend into heaven, He's there. If you make your bed in hell—yep, He's still there. So this isn't about informing God. This is about transforming you.

And let me just say it plainly: Some of us are stuck not because we're not forgiven but because we won't confess. We're walking around with a "just me and God" theology that keeps us isolated, unhealthy, and unhealed. Yes, God forgave you. But healing doesn't flow where hiding still reigns.

You've been in the same cycle for ten, fifteen, twenty years. Why? Because you've kept it all vertical and never brought it horizontal. You've never let safe people in. You've never let the light touch that area. So it stays infected. Quiet. But deadly.

God's grace is not your excuse to avoid transformation. It's your empowerment to step into it. Confession isn't about telling God something He doesn't know—it's about acknowledging the truth so clearly that freedom can finally enter.

Confession says, "That's me. That's where I am. And I don't want to stay here anymore."

So confession isn't about shame. It's about clarity. It's about bringing what's been sitting in the shadows into a place where light can do what light does—reveal and heal.

THE CHURCH'S HIDDEN WAX

In 2025 it felt like every couple of weeks another pastor stepped down. Another scandal. Another press release.

And what grieved me most wasn't the sin itself. It was the spin. "I had a lapse in judgment." "There was a miscommunication." "I fell short of the high standard of Scripture."

Let's call it what it really is.

"I had a lapse in judgment." Maybe that lapse was sexting someone who wasn't your spouse, or using church funds to finance your vacation. That's not a lapse. That's an ethical failure.

"There was a miscommunication." Maybe you said something wildly inappropriate, manipulative, or spiritually abusive. That wasn't a miscommunication. That was misconduct.

"I fell short of the high standard of Scripture." Nah. You committed adultery. You crossed moral lines. You didn't just fall—you dove in and kept swimming.

I wanted someone to say, "I was formed in a toxic environment that never dealt with its own misogyny. I hurt people. I broke trust. And I'm stepping down because this cannot continue."

Or "I built my identity on a platform, not on character. I've been preaching truth I haven't lived, and I'm sitting down—not just to repent, but to recover."

Or even "I manipulated people emotionally and spiritually in the name of 'ministry,' and I'm finally seeing the harm. I'm not leading right now. I'm learning. I'm healing."

I wish more leaders would confess like that.

Because when we don't confess clearly, we confuse the people we're supposed to shepherd. Clear confession from leaders creates trust. Vague confession breeds suspicion. Authentic vulnerability isn't weakness—it's leadership integrity.

There's a story—maybe legend, maybe fact—that the word "sincere" comes from the Latin roots "*sine*" ("without") and "*cera*" ("wax").

Back in ancient Rome, sculptors would use wax to cover flaws in their work. Cracks in marble. Chips in statues. Wax made it look perfect.

Until the heat hit. When the sun came out, the wax melted. The flaws reappeared. And the buyer realized they'd been lied to.[1]

Without wax. Sincere. That's the kind of life I want to live. Not perfect. Not polished. Without wax.

Sincere living isn't about flawlessness—it's about embracing the truth of our humanity openly and honestly, creating space for genuine healing. Because if, instead, we cover up those flaws and try to pretend they're not there, when the heat of life comes—when the lights are bright, the pressure is high, and the platform is raised—that wax won't hold.

I want the real me to be the only version standing when life turns up the heat. Because the truth is we're all cracked somewhere. We've all taken hits. The goal isn't to fake perfection. The goal is to live true. The goal is to be so whole in God that the flaws aren't shameful—they're honest.

What are you using as wax? For some of us, it's work. For others, it's Netflix. Or ministry. Or porn. Or control. Or endless socializing.

Wax isn't always loud. Sometimes it's subtle. Sometimes it's that perfectly curated Instagram feed. That overbooked schedule. That "I'm just busy" line we throw out so we don't have to talk about what's really going on.

Anything can be wax if it's being used to cover up what we don't want to face. Wax is anything we use to hide the cracks instead of healing them.

Some of us inherited wax. Some of us were handed it by leaders, parents, mentors. "Smile for the photo." "Don't let them see you struggle." "Ministry must go on." So we put it on. We polished it up. And then we melted down when life got too hot.

So I have to ask myself these questions:

What am I hiding?
Where do I hurt?
What do I do with that pain?

I can't fix what I won't face. And I can't heal what I'm still covering. If I run from it, it owns me. If I confess it, God meets me in it.

Let's live without wax. Let's be sincere. Even if it means showing the cracks. Because when the light hits those cracks, grace shines through. Grace doesn't demand perfection; it reveals beauty precisely through our broken places. Our cracks aren't disqualifiers—they're conduits of divine healing.

So here's the invitation: Turn on the light.

Not because you need to perform. Not because you need to punish yourself. But because you deserve to see clearly. You deserve to know where you are, what hurts, and what healing looks like.

Confess.

God isn't angry. He isn't shocked. He's waiting: "Thank you for telling Me. I've been here the whole time. Let's heal this. Together."

REFLECTION QUESTIONS

1. Where am I still walking in darkness?
2. What am I trying to navigate without light?
3. What "wax" am I using to hide my flaws?
4. What confession have I been avoiding?
5. What would it look like to live sincere—without wax?

7

LET IT OUT

I've learned something over the years that feels like a quiet revolution in a world full of performance: Telling the truth brings glory to God.

Not the polished, praise-and-worship truth. Not the "I'm blessed and highly favored" truth. I'm talking about the raw, scraped-knees, cracked-voice kind of truth. The kind of truth that makes your throat close up and your palms sweat. The kind of truth that feels dangerous to say out loud but freeing the moment you do. That truth is what brings Him glory.

But here's what I've also learned: That kind of truth doesn't just glorify God—it changes *you*.

When you tell the truth like that, it resets something in your soul. It builds trust with the people around you. It restores dignity, especially when you've fumbled it. Because when someone has experienced you one way—closed off, guarded, inconsistent—and then they watch you get real with them? That's healing in motion. That's honor.

Even if they don't believe in God, they respect the honesty. The humility. The humanity.

That kind of truth creates safety. It earns respect. It builds relationships instead of breaking them.

And that kind of truth—yes, even the trembling kind—turns on the lights. Truth-telling doesn't just honor God; it restores integrity within us, closing the gap between who we pretend to be and who we truly are.

SILENCE CAN BE DEADLY

Joshua's first big win with the Israelites was at Jericho. It was a massive victory. A city with walls so thick you could live in them—gone in seven days. Not one Israelite casualty. That's a miracle.

Next stop? Ai. Smaller city. Fewer people. Should've been light work.

But it wasn't. The Israelites lost. They took a huge *L*. Thirty-six men died, and not in the fight—in the retreat. That's the kind of loss that makes you start questioning everything.

Here's where I want you to pause and see yourself in the story. Have you ever had a Jericho season? A stretch when everything fell into place? When prayers were answered, doors opened, and victories felt effortless? That's Jericho.

But then—Ai.

Something shifted. What should've been simple turned sour. What looked like a guaranteed win became a head-scratching loss. You went from praising on Sunday to panicking by Wednesday. And suddenly you're in the middle of a setback wondering, *What happened?*

That's what Joshua did. He went straight to God: *What happened?*

And God didn't sugarcoat it. "There's sin in the camp."

One man, Achan, had taken what God told the Israelites to leave behind. In the heat of battle, in the thrill of victory, he saw something that caught his eye. A beautiful robe. Some silver. A bar of gold. Things that looked harmless—desirable even. Things God had said *don't touch.* But Achan touched them. He took them. He buried them deep in his tent like nobody would notice. Like it wouldn't matter.

But it did. His silence cost the whole community. And here's the part that gets me: Achan didn't just sin. He stayed silent. He let the people line up by tribe. By family. By household. All while he already knew it was him. They were narrowing it down, casting lots, seeking the truth—and Achan was standing there quiet. Watching. Letting them walk through the whole drawn-out process.

The betrayal wasn't just in the theft. It was in the delay. The denial. The deception. It was the weight he made everyone else carry while he stayed hidden.

Because hidden things don't just burden *you*—they burden *everybody connected to you*. Secrets convince us we're protecting others, but the reality is we're isolating ourselves and creating invisible barriers that prevent authentic connection.

When Joshua finally confronted Achan, he said something that echoes with weight: "Give glory to GOD. . . . Make your confession to him" (Josh. 7:19 MSG).

Not sing louder. Not raise a hallelujah. Not lead a worship night.

Glorify God by telling the truth.

Confession. That's what glorifies God.

That's the moment the weight begins to lift. That's the moment when the hidden no longer holds you hostage. That's the moment freedom becomes possible—for you *and* for the people your silence was slowly suffocating.

Eventually, Achan was punished by being stoned. But Achan

wasn't stoned because he sinned. He was stoned because he lied. Because he hid. Because he let his silence linger long enough to kill other people—and not just any people. His wife. His children. His animals. His entire household paid the price for what he buried in the dirt and refused to confess.

That's what secrets do—they stretch, they suffocate, they spread. You think you're keeping it quiet to protect someone. But you're not preserving them—you're poisoning them. You're making everyone around you carry weight they don't even know they're under.

And that's why confession can't be a last resort. It has to be a first priority.

That goes against our instincts. We're wired for self-preservation. But confession isn't about preserving yourself. It's about liberating yourself. Self-preservation keeps you hidden. Self-liberation brings you into the light. And that shift will save your life. The fear of confession can feel paralyzing—but the liberation that comes from honesty far outweighs the discomfort of the truth being known.

Tell the truth before you're found out. Tell the truth before someone else has to bleed for your silence. Don't wait until the consequences are irreversible. We've got to discipline ourselves to tell the truth even when it makes us look bad. Even when it's going to hurt. Because the truth told early can prevent devastation later.

Get in front of your sin—before your sin gets in front of you. Get in front of your mistake—before your mistake becomes your reputation. Get in front of your wound—before your silence lets it fester. Get in front of your pattern, your dysfunction, your hidden habit—before it gets broadcast without your permission.

Not everything is a sin. But if it's sitting in the dark and shaping how you show up in the world, it still needs to be confessed. Whether it's failure, fear, pride, or pain—own it before it owns you.

CONFESSION REGULATES THE SOUL

Did you know that confession regulates the soul? I've seen this firsthand, in my life and in others'. Over and over again.

As I mentioned earlier, when I was nineteen years old, I confessed to my parents that I had been sexually abused when I was eight. I bring it up again here because of what it illustrates. That confession didn't just bring clarity—it brought *oxygen* back to my body. It was like my lungs finally remembered how to breathe. And it reminds me every time that confession isn't a one-time event—it's a lifestyle of release, of realignment, of healing.

But that wasn't the only time I had to confess. I had to confess that I brought my porn addiction into my marriage with Juliette. I had to confess when I relapsed—even after I was supposedly "walking in freedom." I had to confess when I was wrong in arguments. When I got petty. When I got prideful. When I got out-of-pocket.

And I remember one of the most humbling confessions of my life: In 2019 I spray-painted words on the walls of our church building. I had asked for those words to be painted for two years. Nothing happened. So one day I just did it myself—with a spray can. It was an act of defiance masked as creativity. I was convicted two days later while reading the book of Exodus. Of all the books that could have convicted me, it was Exodus. That next Sunday happened to be Communion at our church. I stood up, not just to tell the truth but to confess. I didn't dress it up. I said what I did was wrong. And when I did, I was free. The weight lifted. The tension broke. I walked off that platform lighter than I had felt in months.

When I hold something in, my body knows. My chest tightens. My mood shifts. My nervous system buzzes like a broken wire. It doesn't matter if the secret is old or new—my body keeps score. And silence only turns up the volume.

But when I speak it out? When I confess vertically to God and horizontally to a safe community? It's like the windows of my soul fly open. Like a fresh wind blows through and sweeps out the debris. My mind stops racing. The static in my brain fades. My thoughts settle. My nervous system stops firing false alarms and starts regulating. Breath returns—not shallow, anxious breath, but deep, grounded breath that reminds me I'm safe now. My heart stops pounding. The tension in my shoulders eases. And spiritually? It's like the connection between me and God gets cleared of static. His voice becomes easier to hear. His presence, easier to feel. Confession does that. It clears space in the mind, calms the body, and restores clarity to the soul.

Confession moves us from a state of internal chaos into regulated calm, helping our nervous systems realize we're no longer living under the threat of being found out. Because confession isn't just moral. It's neurological. It's physiological. It's spiritual. It brings alignment to our souls, to our nervous systems, and to our connections with God and others.

GOING DEEPER

There's a difference between saying, "I struggle with lust," and saying, "I'm maintaining a relationship with someone I haven't told anyone about. It's gone too far, and I'm scared of what that says about me."

There's a difference between saying, "I stress eat," and saying, "I binge in secret because it numbs me for a while, and I'm afraid if I stop, I'll have to feel what I've been avoiding."

There's a difference between saying, "I'm tired," and saying, "I feel numb most days, and I'm afraid I'm starting to detach from my life."

There's a difference between saying, "I've been frustrated with my spouse," and saying, "I've been fantasizing about someone else because I don't know how to deal with the distance that's grown between us."

There's a difference between saying, "I've been spending a lot lately," and saying, "I've been trying to buy my way out of sadness with new shoes, new gadgets, and the rush that comes with every delivery notification."

There's a difference between saying, "I think I have trust issues," and saying, "Every time someone gets close, I sabotage it because I'm terrified they'll leave like everyone else has."

There's a difference between saying, "I procrastinate a lot," and saying, "I avoid starting things I care about because failing at something that matters feels way more painful than succeeding at something that doesn't."

Surface confession is like skimming leaves off the top of a pool.

Real confession is diving to the bottom and pulling out the bricks.

We don't just need to confess the fruit—we need to find the root. That takes honesty. That takes attunement. That takes language.

We have more words for our fruits than we do for our roots. We've been taught how to name the behavior but not how to name the belief behind it. We can describe the symptom but not the source. We've rehearsed the cover story so many times that we forgot to learn the language of what's underneath it all.

Healing begins where truth gets specific. Surface-level confession alleviates temporary guilt; deep confession transforms lasting shame. Real healing requires vulnerability beneath the convenient stories we've learned to tell.

I'm not writing this book because I have it all figured out. I'm writing it because I've been the guy who hid. The guy who lied. The guy who allowed low self-esteem, low self-worth, and people-pleasing to minimize my voice most times and completely silence it at other times. I'm writing because I've lived in the prison of performance and the cave of secrecy.

Someone once told me after I vulnerably shared my story, "You give people the gift of going second." That line has stayed with me ever since. It wrecked me—in the best way. Because to give someone the gift of going second, you have to be willing to go first.

That's what this is. That's why I'm telling all of it. That's why I'm putting myself on blast, sharing embarrassing moments and uncomfortable truths. Not because I like pain but because I want you to go second. And then I want someone to go third. And someone else to go fourth. Fifth. Sixth. Seventh. Eighth. Ninth. Tenth.

So if I have to go first, I'm doing it with open hands and a steady heart. I'm doing it to make space. I'm doing it to show you what it looks like when shame loses and freedom wins.

I want to give you the gift of going second. That's why I'm going first. Vulnerability is contagious—and courageous honesty inspires others to move from secrecy to freedom. Every truth told weakens shame's grip.

And I am honored to go first for you.

WEARING WHITE

Ever worn all white to an event?

You move differently. You avoid toddlers with juice boxes. You sidestep grass stains. You do hourly body checks, like "Am I still clean?"

That's what confession does. It raises your awareness. You walk differently when you know you're being honest. When you're not carrying secrets. You step lighter. You speak freer. You listen better. Because the weight is off your chest and off your mind.

You don't need to wear black to hide the mess. You don't need to dress up your anxiety in productivity. Or your lust in jokes. Or your depression in sarcasm. You don't need to clothe your loneliness in busyness. Or your insecurity in name-dropping. Or your bitterness in fake laughter. We're out here layering up emotions like spiritual shapewear, hoping nobody sees the real contours of our souls.

Let me say this clearly: I'm not coming after your wardrobe. You can wear whatever color you want. But emotionally? Spiritually? Relationally? I want you in white.

It doesn't matter what you've got on the outside if the inside is buried under secrets.

Spiritual honesty isn't just about avoiding sin; it's about cultivating an internal environment where shame cannot thrive and authenticity naturally flourishes.

We want to be clean. Inside. Honest. Whole.

Come in white.

Come exposed.

God already knows what's there. He's not looking to shame you. He's offering you a mirror, saying, "Let's deal with this together."

EXERCISING CONFESSION

Confession is easier said than done. Dishonesty is our default. We don't learn it. We are born with it. Ask any four-year-old with cookie crumbs on their face.

Confession is learned. Trained. Practiced.

It goes against our instinct to self-protect. Our instinct to hide is rooted in fear; learning to confess openly rewrites those instincts toward trust and relational safety.

That's why I say confession is like a first-responder skill. It takes guts. It takes running toward the fire inside you instead of away from it.

But it also saves lives. Yours included.

So how do we get past our natural instinct to lie and move into confession? Let me break down the three steps I've practiced over the years.

STEP 1: GET HONEST WITH YOURSELF

Stop lying. That's the first move. But don't stop there—start truthing. I know that's not technically a word, but it should be. Stop lying and start truthing. Tell the truth, even if it's hard. Even if it's messy. Even if it makes you look bad.

For example:

You know Friday is your worst workday. Stop pretending it's not. Rework your schedule.

You know alcohol is wrecking your marriage. Stop saying it's not a problem.

You know you're snapping at your kids because you haven't dealt with your own inner child. Start naming that.

You know you're afraid of slowing down because you've tied your worth to your productivity. Say that.

You know you're still hurt by what they said five years ago—even though you "moved on." Admit that.

Recognize the pattern. Name it. Own it. Because nothing heals until it's real.

STEP 2: COME INTO AGREEMENT WITH GOD

This is the part where I go to Scripture and say, "What does God say about this?" Because no matter what you're going through, there is a word in God's Word for your situation. You need to find the book, the chapter, and the verse. Something you can stand on. Recite. Repeat. Memorize. Pray through. Let it soak into your bones until it changes how you think and how you live.

Here are some examples. Do you need to come into agreement with God about . . .

- rest? "Remember the Sabbath day, to keep it holy" (Exod. 20:8). Rest isn't a suggestion—it's a command with a blessing attached to it.
- drunkenness? "Don't be drunk with wine, because that will ruin your life" (Eph. 5:18 NLT).
- anxiety? "Be anxious for nothing. . . . The peace of God . . . will guard your hearts and minds" (Phil. 4:6–7).
- pride? "Pride goes before destruction, and a haughty spirit before a fall" (Prov. 16:18).

Agreement with God brings clarity. But clarity is possible only when you're willing to align your opinions, feelings, and impulses with His truth. You may never see your addiction, your struggle, or your choices the way God sees them—and that's why He has to be Lord. You don't get freedom by calling it what you want; you get free by calling it what *He* says it is.

STEP 3: INTERNALIZE AND VERBALIZE

This is where I say, "God, I see it. I hate that I've been avoiding it. I want to be free. Help me walk this out."

It's not performance. It's partnership.

You might not always *feel* what God feels about your issue—but you can *agree* with Him. And when you agree with Him, even when you don't fully understand, you allow His truth to start transforming your reality.

Y'all! My mom walked in on me watching porn. It was humiliating. But it was also liberating. Because that moment cracked the silence wide open. I told her the truth. Not just about the behavior—but about the pain behind it.

And something shifted.

Confession isn't just about admitting wrong—it's about inviting right. It's stepping into alignment with God's truth so fully that shame loses its power over your story.

TELLING THE TRUTH DOESN'T GROW THE SIN—IT SHRINKS IT

Some folks say, "Don't confess it! Don't give it power!"

I disagree. Strongly.

I've heard all the warnings. Don't say it out loud—it'll be used against you. Don't write it down—someone might find it. Don't admit it—just pray it away. And then there's the extra-spiritual layer of glitter they throw on it: "Don't confess it—you're giving it power." That's not Scripture. That's superstition.

Here's what I know: The more I confessed, the smaller my addiction got. The less power it held. The more peace I had. The more whole I became. I was fully seen, fully heard, fully known—and still fully loved.

That's what telling the truth does. It doesn't feed the sin—it starves it.

Satan wants you to lie to yourself. To say you're fine. To spiritualize your silence. To hide behind praise reports while bleeding in private. That's how he keeps you stuck.

God wants your truth. Your honesty. Your surrender. And He's not coming to punish—He's coming to heal.

Some of us grew up in family systems where keeping it in the family was gospel. Where silence was loyalty. Where confession was called "snitching," and secrets were a form of survival. But what protected you back then is poisoning you now. Confession isn't betrayal. It's breakthrough. Confession disrupts generational patterns of secrecy, creating a legacy of transparency, emotional health, and authentic faith.

So I'll say it plain: Confession is good for the soul. "The truth will set you free" (John 8:32 NLT).

I'm telling mine so you can tell yours.

REFLECTION QUESTIONS

1. What secret have I been carrying that needs to come into the light?
2. Where have I been doing surface-level confession instead of bottom-of-the-heart honesty?
3. What habit or behavior am I still trying to justify?
4. What would it look like to tell the truth today?
5. Whom could I safely share it with?

8

HORIZONTAL CONFESSION

Confessing to God is essential—no question. That vertical alignment is where peace starts.

But it doesn't end there.

If I want to be healthy and fully seen, heard, known, and loved—even if not always understood—then I need to learn the art of horizontal confession. That means confessing to other people. Not just in a vague "I'm struggling" way. I'm talking real-life, say-it-out-loud, bring-it-into-the-light confession.

And I know that can feel terrifying. Horizontal confession isn't just about transparency; it's about trust. It deepens relationships and turns communities into sanctuaries of healing.

"WHY DO I NEED TO TELL ANYONE ELSE?"

I get that question a lot.

"Tim, I just confessed everything to God. We had a full-on moment. I cried. I repented. He forgave me. Why do I need to bring it to my wife? To a therapist? To my mentor or best friend? Why dig it up again?"

Here's the answer: because God designed us for connection.

In Genesis 2:18, God said, "It is not good that man should be alone." That's not just a marital statement. That is a relational statement. Period. We weren't meant to carry the full weight of our humanity by ourselves.

Even Jesus didn't roll solo. Let's break that down.

As a child, He submitted to His parents. Not because they were perfect but because He understood the value of authority and relational structure. As an adult, He didn't isolate—He built community. He walked closely with twelve other men. He spent intentional time with them, taught them, broke bread with them. And not only that—He had His inner circle. On the mountaintop and in the garden, He brought Peter, James, and John. Those were His "go with Me when it's heavy" kind of people.

The *only* time Jesus was truly alone was on the cross. And that wasn't by choice—it was by calling. Because no one else could carry that burden but Him.

So let's keep it real—if Jesus, the Son of God, leaned in to connection, then how dare I try to walk out my healing alone?

If Jesus chose community, I *need* to choose it too. If He invited others into His sorrow and joy, why would I think isolation is more spiritual?

If Jesus chose connection, I *should* too. And not just as a backup plan but as a blueprint. Isolation might promise safety, but connection provides sanctuary—where burdens are shared, not hidden, and wounds heal in the open air of relationship.

HEALING HAPPENS IN COMMUNITY

First John 1:9 says that when I confess my sins to God, He forgives and cleanses me. That's vertical.

But James 5:16 says, "Confess your sins to each other and pray for each other so that you may be healed" (NLT).

Did you catch that?

God forgives. Community heals.

I can be forgiven and still not be free. I can be cleansed and still not be whole.

I know believers who have confessed to God every day for years and still carry the same trauma, the same shame, the same behavioral loops. Why? Because they never shared it with someone who could walk with them toward healing. God's forgiveness removes the eternal penalty of sin, but community confession dismantles the earthly power that shame holds over us.

Let's get honest. Who knows about the thing you keep going back to? The habit, the pattern, the secret? You can confess it to God, and He'll absolutely meet you with grace. But if no one else knows—if no one else can check on you, pray with you, or speak life into you when the temptation hits again—you're setting yourself up to stay stuck.

I know this because I used to keep secrets. I know that space. I lived there. And here's what I've learned: Something different happens when you look another person in the face and tell them the truth. It does something to your soul. It humbles you. It grounds you. It invites accountability in a way that vertical confession alone doesn't. Don't just confess in private. Confess in partnership. That's where transformation lives. The truth spoken to another person isn't just accountability—it's advocacy. You're inviting someone into your story, empowering them to support your healing journey.

So yeah, somebody else has to know. Somebody besides God has to know—because if no one else knows, you're probably not coming up out of it. I'm just keeping it real. If no one's checking your blind spots, if no one's helping you carry the weight, then freedom will always stay just out of reach. If you're going to be free, you've got to be honest. And not just with God. Healing happens in the light. Every confession to another person is a declaration of trust, not just in that person, but in the healing power of community itself.

USE YOUR WORDS

I remember what settled in my spirit at nineteen after I confessed to my mom for the first time: I never wanted to live with another secret again.

That conviction has never left me.

Because you can't heal what you won't reveal. Period.

I tell my boys all the time, "Whatever doesn't come up and out of your mouth through words will come up and out of your body through actions." One of my therapists said it like this: "Your mind needs words to heal." And there's a book that says it plainly: *The Body Keeps the Score* by Bessel van der Kolk. That title alone is a whole sermon. Because it's true—your body remembers what your mouth avoids.

So if your body is the scoreboard, your mouth is the announcer. The scoreboard tells you what's happening, but the announcer gives you the story behind the stats. You need both. You need to know the count, and you need the context.

When I keep everything inside, it festers. My nervous system gets stuck in overdrive. I get edgy, reactive, exhausted. I act out what my mouth refuses to name.

But when I speak up? When I give words to the weight? My body exhales. My brain settles. My spirit lifts. That's why confession isn't just emotional—it's neurological. It's spiritual. It's physical. It's a full-body reset.

Confession breaks the cycle and resets the rhythm. Naming trauma and struggles aloud to another trusted person reduces their physiological hold, giving your nervous system permission to reset into calmness.

HORIZONTAL CONFESSION AT HOME

One of the best gifts I can give my kids—and my family as a whole—is a healed version of me. Not a perfect version. Not a performative version. A *healed* one. I want to pass down wisdom, not wounds. I want to normalize confession so they grow up thinking truth-telling is strength, not weakness.

This is one of the sneak parenting hacks that most folks miss: Regulating yourself helps you become emotionally available to regulate your kids. Confession isn't just a vertical tool for your spirit; it's a relational one for your home. So when I see one of my sons acting out, I don't just react. I pause. I check in. I say, "You're dysregulated. Let's talk." Nine times out of ten, it's not just misbehavior; it's a message. Sometimes my sons don't even know what they're feeling until we name it together. That's parenting. That's discipleship. That's trauma-informed leadership under your own roof.

I'm not trying to raise emotionally suppressed performers. I'm trying to raise whole, grounded men who know how to name what's happening in their bodies and hearts. That starts with how I respond to their hardest moments.

That's horizontal confession in a family setting. It's not just "confessing sins"—it's creating a safe space to say the hard stuff. No shame. No punishment first. Just honest processing, modeled out loud.

When my boys see me owning my moments, they learn how to own theirs. That's legacy. That's healing passed down. Generational healing happens when transparency becomes a household norm, replacing cycles of secrecy with legacies of openness and emotional health.

HORIZONTAL CONFESSION AT WORK AND IN FRIENDSHIP

Horizontal confession works with peers too. It works on teams, in circles, and with close friends who are willing to keep it honest and grounded.

Sometimes I sit down with my team and ask, "How are you experiencing me right now? This week? This season?"

That one question can unlock a whole world of awareness. It's not about micromanaging people's opinions of me—it's about being curious enough to care how my presence is affecting the people I lead and love.

Imagine if more friendships had that kind of humility baked in. Imagine asking your closest friend, "What is it like to have a friend like me?" That's a different level of self-awareness. That's someone who's trying to grow, not just to be liked.

Yes, it's vulnerable. Yes, it's risky. But it builds trust.

They might say, "You seem distracted." "You've been hard to read." "You feel joyful lately."

Whatever it is, I listen. I don't defend. I don't dismiss. I sit with it. I lean in to it. Not because I always agree with their perceptions but because I value the gift of their perspectives.

I may not see it the way they see it, but I honor the fact that that's how they're experiencing me. And that makes me more self-aware, more grounded, more whole. And honestly? That's just a better way to live. Real friendship and leadership flourish where authenticity is normalized and feedback isn't just tolerated—it's invited as a catalyst for growth.

CALL YOUR OWN FOULS

Basketball is my favorite sport. I like the way the players dribble up and down the court (did anybody get it?). Lakers for life. But let me tell you what I can't stand: I can't stand the players who get called for a foul and turn around with their mouths wide open, looking shocked. Appalled. Like "Who, *me*?" Yes. *You*. You fouled him. This is a contact sport. Bodies are flying everywhere. Your arm's still in his chest, and you're surprised?

Now flip it: I *love* the players who keep it real. The ones who commit a foul and throw up their hands before the whistle even blows. Like their bodies already knew what their spirits were saying: *"That was on me."* They double-tap their chests, make eye contact with the other player, and own it. That's my jam. That's integrity in motion.

And that's how I want to live. I want to be someone who calls my own fouls. Who says, "Yep, that was me. I got angry. I snapped. I went too far. I need help."

Not because I got caught. Because I value healing.

I'm not trying to be caught. I'm trying to be *kept*. And one of the ways I stay kept? I call my own fouls.

That's what I'm trying to normalize. That's what I'm building my life on: owning my story—the good, the bad, and the ugly. That's where freedom lives. Owning our mistakes quickly doesn't just restore integrity—it strengthens trust. It communicates that we value connection more than pride. You're going to mess up. That's part of the human experience. But the goal isn't perfection. It's awareness. And one of the clearest paths to awareness is accountability.

Now, let me be clear: Accountability is not parole (I go into great detail about this in the next chapter). I grew up in a time when having an accountability partner meant someone called you every Friday and asked four scripted questions: "Did you look at porn? Did you lie about anything? Did you read your Bible? Did you pray?" Listen, that's not accountability. That's probation with a Bible verse.

Real accountability isn't someone checking up on you—it's *you* checking in with someone else. It's voluntary. It's intentional. It's ownership.

So build a rhythm of checking in with your spouse, a therapist, a trusted friend, or a spiritual mentor. And don't wait until you're drowning. You don't have to schedule a full conversation every time. Leave a voice note. Send a text. Fire off a quick "Hey, I'm in a moment. Can you pray for me?"

Sometimes just saying something—anything—is enough to interrupt the spiral.

That's how I've stayed free. Not because people were chasing me down but because I made a decision to keep myself in check. I was the one doing the reaching out. I turned it into a rhythm. A discipline.

Practice saying, "Here's what I'm carrying. Here's where I'm struggling. Can you walk with me?" You'll be surprised how healing those moments can be. Because freedom thrives where honesty lives. True accountability is proactive and relational, creating a safe container where confession is a bridge to connection, not a badge of shame.

REFLECTION QUESTIONS

1. What would healing in community look like for me?
2. Who in my life feels safe enough to hear my horizontal confession?
3. Am I using my words to express what's going on inside, or waiting for my behaviors to act it out?
4. How are others experiencing me right now?
5. Have I called my own fouls lately?

9

IT'S ALL ABOUT ACCOUNTABILITY

Accountability gets misrepresented a lot these days. Some people think it means spilling your business all over social media—as though that somehow equals transparency. But posting your lowest moments to a crowd of strangers isn't accountability. That's exposure without support. That's vulnerability without safety.

Real accountability isn't about going viral with your confession. It's about going deeper with your healing.

Real accountability builds a support system around your soul. It creates relationships where others know your triggers, your patterns, and your pain points—and still choose to walk with you.

Real accountability transforms vulnerability from a threat into a pathway to deeper connection and genuine healing.

TELL THE RIGHT PEOPLE

When temptation rises, when your thoughts get cloudy, when your heart starts to wander, you don't need to tell the world. You need to tell someone who knows how to hold your pain without weaponizing it.

Because when I speak something out to someone I trust, it loses power.

But let me say this as clearly as I can: Not everyone qualifies to hear your confession. Not everyone is worthy of your vulnerability. Just because someone is available doesn't mean they're trustworthy. Just because they're nearby doesn't mean they're safe.

I've seen people pour their hearts out to someone who couldn't hold water—and it did more damage than good. If you're trying to live with integrity, you need to be walking with people who live with integrity. Period.

Accountability isn't about unloading truth to just anybody. It's about sharing with the right people—the ones who know how to honor your honesty, hold your story, and walk with you, not talk about you.

So, yes, tell someone. But tell the right someone. When we carefully choose the people who hear our truth, confession becomes a step toward wholeness, not another source of wounding.

ACCOUNTABILITY IS NOT PAROLE

As I mentioned in the previous chapter, accountability is not parole—and I need to double down on that.

I've seen the church treat accountability like parole. Check-ins every Friday. Four questions. Scripted conversations. Maybe even a spreadsheet. That's not healing. That's a monitoring system dressed up in religious language. Accountability isn't about surveillance. It's about support. It's not "Prove you're clean." It's "Let's walk together through the mess."

Real accountability requires relationship. It means someone knows my rhythms—the good days and the hard days. It means someone can ask me hard questions and offer soft landings. It changed everything for me when I invited real people into my struggle. When I could look Juliette in the eyes and say, "I failed," it did something holy. Not easy. Holy.

Because the look on her face grounded me in the reality that my choices affected more people than just me. Healthy accountability reminds me I'm not alone—it anchors me in relationships that care enough to reflect both my struggles and my worth. When I had to sit across from someone and own my behavior, I couldn't hide behind theology or excuses. I had to be honest. I had to be seen.

And there was something healing in that. Because shame hides. But accountability exposes—for the sake of restoration.

It's one thing to admit something in your prayer closet. It's another thing to look another person in the face and say, "That was me." That's a mirror moment. That's when you see yourself clearly—not just who you were trying to be, but who you actually are in that moment. And when someone else sees it, too, and still holds space for you? That's where the shame starts to melt.

Accountability isn't parole. It doesn't just reveal where you fell short—it reminds you that you're not disqualified by it. It gives you a new path forward. It tells you, "You're still here. And you're still becoming." When accountability holds up the mirror, it does more than just show flaws—it reveals resilience and invites growth.

DISCIPLESHIP > PAROLE

Somewhere along the way we started emphasizing accountability and forgot about discipleship. Jesus didn't check in with His disciples once a week and ask, "Did you sin today?"

He walked with them.

He laughed with them.

He taught them.

He challenged them.

He sat with them in sorrow and celebrated with them in joy.

That's the model. That's the blueprint.

Let's take Peter, for example. In Matthew 16, Peter got bold—too bold—and tried to tell Jesus what He would and wouldn't do. Jesus didn't wait a week to deal with it. He corrected Peter on the spot: "Get away from me, Satan! You are a dangerous trap to me. You are seeing things merely from a human point of view, not from God's" (v. 23 NLT). That's discipleship in action—loving correction that happens in real time because of proximity.

Later, Jesus told Peter, "Satan has asked for you, that he may sift you as wheat. But I have prayed for you, that your faith should not fail; and when you have returned to Me, strengthen your brethren" (Luke 22:31–32). That's accountability with compassion. That's correction anchored in relationship. Jesus wasn't monitoring Peter—He was mentoring him. He was discipling him.

That kind of proximity doesn't happen over once-a-month coffee. You don't see spiritual shifts and character arcs from a distance. You have to walk together. Eat together. Sweat together. Pray together.

If I meet with someone once a month for an hour, that's mentorship. That's coaching. And it can be good—it has its place. But discipleship? That's different. That costs more. It costs time. Proximity. Emotional investment. It's not transactional—it's transformational. And if Jesus, the perfect Son of God, modeled discipleship over parole, so should we.

True discipleship builds bridges of trust strong enough to bear the weight of honest conversations, real-time correction, and genuine growth.

I've seen people try to hold others accountable without being invested. That's not accountability. That's control. My niece is a parole officer. She does her job well. But she doesn't know the full lives of the people she supervises. She checks boxes. She measures compliance. That's not what I need from a friend, a mentor, or a brother in Christ. I don't need someone checking my behavior—I need someone checking on my heart.

And let's be clear: Without relational equity, trust just isn't there. You can't build depth with someone you don't actually know. You can't correct someone you haven't consistently cared for. Accountability without trust is just control wearing a church lanyard.

We're not looking for people to manage our behavior—we're looking for relationships in which we can be fully seen, fully heard, fully known, and fully loved. That's the goal. That's what makes accountability safe and sustainable.

I need someone who sees me, hears me, and knows me and still chooses to walk with me. That's what real accountability looks like. Accountability built on genuine relationship ensures that the correction we receive heals rather than harms, uplifts rather than undermines.

Now, let me say this: I know trust gets broken. And when it does? It hurts. That feeling of betrayal cuts deep.

Maybe you told someone your truth and they spread it.

Maybe they judged you.

Maybe they didn't hold it well.

And so you decided, "That's why I don't tell people anything."

First of all, I get it. I really do. That pain is real. And I'm sorry. But that wasn't accountability. That was betrayal. And we can't let betrayal build the blueprint for how we do relationships going forward. We cannot globalize our pain. There are eight billion people out there. And somewhere among them is someone capable of holding your truth with care, honor, and humility. Someone who knows how to steward what you give them and won't weaponize your vulnerability.

Yes, trust takes time. Yes, it takes discernment. But it's still possible. Don't shut down because of what happened with a few. Don't let a bad experience become your whole worldview. Healing still happens in community. But only if you're willing to try again. Trust broken doesn't have to become trust permanently lost—it can become wisdom gained, guiding you toward safer relationships.

Trust is still possible. There are still good people. Safe people. Trustworthy people. Don't let a few bad experiences convince you that protection means isolation.

SOMETIMES THE CIRCLE CHANGES

Sometimes accountability doesn't work because the people around me are no longer right for me.

Maybe I've grown and they haven't.

Maybe I've pursued healing and they're still living in dysfunction.

Maybe I'm finding peace and they're still drawn to chaos.

That doesn't make them bad people.

That just means I need new people.

I remember dating someone before I got saved. I met her in the club. She was there to have a good time. I was too—but I was also looking for something more. So we started dating. And once we were together, I didn't want to go back to the club. I wanted to build something deeper. But she wasn't ready to leave that life. She wanted someone to stay in the scene with her. I was looking to get out.

So what brought us together—the club—couldn't keep us together. And eventually we parted ways.

You can be brought together in one season of your life, and that season can shift—for you, or for them. If there's no open communication, if there's no mutual growth or maturity, the gap gets wider.

Growth changes things.

And sometimes, when the circle stops growing with you, it's time to find a new one. Recognizing when your circle needs to shift isn't rejection—it's self-respect and spiritual discernment in action.

I was thinking about this when I watched Christian people online get wrecked over the 2024 Paris Olympics opening ceremony. There was imagery that didn't sit well with a lot of Christians. And I get it. Kinda.

Here's what I don't get: expecting the world to act like the church.

Jesus didn't do that.

He didn't stand in front of Pilate and say, "You're not acting saved enough." He didn't throw stones at the Roman guards. He didn't spend His days fighting empire symbolism online. He didn't hold culture to a covenant it never agreed to.

If I find myself constantly dysregulated by what people outside the faith are doing, it might not be about their behavior—it might be about my focus.

Maybe I need to shift my circle. Refocus my energy. Recenter my attention.

Because outrage is not a fruit of the Spirit. Peace is. Patience is. Kindness is. Self-control is.

Let's stop trying to make the culture look like the church—and start making the church look like Jesus. True accountability in the church doesn't project our convictions onto culture; it reflects Christ's character through compassionate relationships and honest conversations. And if I want accountability to work, I need the right people around me.

Maybe that means finding a new coffee shop.

Maybe it means saying goodbye to the friends I used to party with.

Maybe it means starting therapy.

Maybe it means leaving the group chat on silent and creating new rhythms around new relationships.

I'm not stuck with the first group I opened up to. Just because they were there in one season doesn't mean they belong in every season.

There are four seasons: winter, spring, summer, and fall. And not everyone is equipped to walk with you through all of them. Some folks are your snow-day friends—great in the cold, but not built for the heat. Others are sunshine people—fun in the summer, but nowhere to be found when life gets heavy. That doesn't make them bad. That just makes them seasonal.

You've got to discern the difference between lifelong companions and seasonal companions. And you've got to be honest enough to know when the season has changed.

There are very few four-season friends. So when someone doesn't show up well in your summer, but they were your rock in the winter, thank God for the season they walked with you—and then keep walking.

Accountability thrives in safety. And safety requires intention. Sometimes growth demands we reevaluate our circles. It doesn't mean we're better than anyone. It just means we're called to be better for ourselves—and better equipped for all the seasons to come. Switching circles isn't selfish—it's stewardship. It's recognizing the sacredness of your healing journey and protecting it intentionally.

When I'm around people who are invested in my growth—not just my image—I can confess without fear. I can stumble without being shamed. I can bring my full self to the table and still be met with grace.

That kind of community takes time to build. It takes effort. It takes trust built slowly over consistent integrity. But it's worth the work.

Because who you tell—who you invite into your healing process—will shape how deeply and how freely you heal. When accountability is thoughtfully chosen, the healing that follows isn't just deep—it's sustainable, life-giving, and lasting.

REFLECTION QUESTIONS

1. What is true accountability to me?
2. Who in my life is safe enough to hold my truth?
3. Have I mistaken parole for real support?
4. Is there anyone I need to release because our paths have diverged?
5. Am I willing to build a new circle in which healing and honesty can thrive?

10

UNSPOKEN

We're almost there.

If you've been journeying with me through this book, let's pause right here. You're doing profoundly courageous work. This hasn't been casual or comfortable reading. You've faced silence head-on, grappled openly with confession, confronted maladaptive behaviors, and stared into trauma's lingering shadows. You've seen hard truths and chosen to stay. That matters. This is genuine, transformative work.

Before we dive deeper into the heart surgery ahead, let's discuss one crucial element of horizontal confession that might be silently undermining your healing.

IF YOU'RE NOT TALKING, YOU'RE NOT HEALING

If I don't speak it, *you* can't pray for it.

Simple but profound. Silence can feel safer—it temporarily protects us from immediate vulnerability, judgment, or misunderstanding. But that safety is an illusion, and it comes at a steep cost. Silence erects barriers that isolate us, cutting off not only the healing we crave but also the vital support we urgently need.

Let's consider this cost in detail. Spiritually, silence keeps us disconnected from the precise, intentional prayers of others. It prevents our community from interceding specifically on our behalf. Imagine a soldier on a battlefield refusing to communicate exact coordinates to his support team. Without clear communication, support cannot be accurately deployed, leaving the soldier vulnerable and isolated. Spiritually, our silence similarly denies us precise intercession, leaving us spiritually vulnerable and less able to fend off attacks, whether they come in the form of temptation, doubt, or fear.

Emotionally, silence fuels shame. The longer we conceal our struggles, the heavier they become. Shame festers in silence—it grows stronger, more corrosive, and more entrenched. Each unspoken struggle adds weight, intensifying anxiety, depression, loneliness, and fear. Our emotions become bottled up, increasing stress and reducing our capacity for joy, peace, and genuine connection.

Relationally, silence erodes trust and intimacy. Authentic relationships require vulnerability and transparency. Without openness, relationships stagnate at a superficial level, built on partial truths and incomplete connections. People sense the distance, even if they don't fully understand why. Over time, relationships deteriorate, unable to withstand the weight of hidden struggles.

Physiologically, research confirms that chronic emotional suppression and isolation negatively affect our bodies. Unaddressed stress and emotional burdens can lead to elevated cortisol levels, resulting in impaired immune responses, increased heart rate, disrupted sleep patterns, digestive issues, and chronic fatigue. The body keeps score—when our emotional and spiritual truths remain unspoken, our physical health inevitably suffers.

Think about it this way: Would you continue a financial habit if an accountant showed you exactly how much money you were losing each month? Probably not. Similarly, if you understood the spiritual, emotional, relational, and physiological toll silence exacts, why would you consciously still choose it?

James 5:16 speaks with undeniable clarity: "Confess your faults one to another, and pray one for another, that ye may be healed. The effectual fervent prayer of a righteous man availeth much" (KJV).

Healing thrives on honesty. Power emerges from precision. Generalities invite only general help. Specificity invites profound breakthroughs.

Let's deeply internalize this truth: Clear confession unites hearts in purposeful, targeted prayer. Specific prayer requests transform vague sympathy into actionable, potent support. Vague prayers evaporate quickly, but clear, targeted prayers strike like arrows, breaking through the barriers of shame and isolation, ushering in genuine healing and lasting transformation.

PRAYER NEEDS 411, NOT VIBES

Effective prayer isn't just good vibes—it's like an air strike: precise, targeted, and powerful. It requires clear intel to hit the heart of what you're battling. Without clarity, praying is more like throwing darts blindfolded; you might hit something, but probably not what truly needs attention.

Remember dialing 411 before Google owned the information game? (Yeah, I'm older than you think.) You'd call up, ask for exactly what you needed—a specific phone number or address—and, boom, you got direct intel without any guesswork. No flipping through thick Yellow Pages, no going down rabbit trails, just quick, precise information. That's exactly how our prayer life should feel.

Your prayer requests should have that same kind of directness. If anxiety's got you locked in your room doomscrolling at 3:00 a.m., let somebody know that. If you're on the edge of relapsing into self-harm, speak up. If lust, rage, codependency, or substance use is creeping back, be explicit. Don't sugarcoat or talk around it. Put a clear target on what you're facing so your people can intercede powerfully and purposefully.

Here's the real: Vague prayers get vague responses. Specific prayers set off alarms in heaven, rally your community, and equip everyone to go to war on your behalf. Detailed confessions give your squad clear coordinates, helping them aim their prayers like guided missiles, bringing authentic relief, real comfort, and lasting transformation.

THE DANGER OF "UNSPOKEN" PRAYER CULTURE

I grew up in church hearing, "Does anyone have an unspoken prayer request?" Hands would quietly go up around the room. It seemed polite, respectful, and safe, but that silence came at a huge cost.

What we don't reveal, we can't heal.

The idea of keeping things unspoken was passed down from a generation literally referred to as the "Silent Generation," folks who grew up in the shadows of war, hardship, and strict social expectations.[1] They learned early to hide their pain, to tuck away secrets, and to endure quietly, carrying burdens privately to their graves. This legacy of silence leaked into our churches, our homes, our marriages, and, ultimately, our hearts.

Here's the thing about silence—it breeds isolation. Isolation feeds shame. And shame pushes us deeper into secrecy, creating a vicious cycle that locks us away from the community we desperately need. The longer we stay silent, the deeper shame embeds itself, twisting how we see ourselves and others, making the possibility of healing seem unreachable and support feel impossible.

Breaking this pattern requires guts. It takes courage to let your voice shake, to speak truths that might make others uncomfortable, and to step into vulnerability. But when you voice your struggles, something powerful happens. Shame loses its grip. Community gets activated. Connection becomes real. Naming our pain aloud doesn't just make us feel better—it creates solidarity, empathy, and avenues for healing.

Imagine the weight lifting off your shoulders when you stop hiding behind polite smiles and vague statements. Picture the freedom that comes when you openly share your struggle. This isn't just emotional relief—it's transformative freedom. Authentic confession dismantles generational chains, shatters isolation, and rebuilds our lives with honesty, transparency, and healing power.

GENERATIONAL CURSES?

We often talk about generational curses as mystical or deeply spiritual burdens—forces beyond our control haunting families generation after generation. But what if I told you that some (or most) of these curses might actually just be bad intel—unspoken, unshared family secrets quietly transmitted through time, never clearly named or openly discussed?

Depression, anxiety, addiction, loneliness—what we call curses are often just inherited silences, family dysfunctions passed down not through blood or mystical forces but through a profound lack of open, transparent communication. When these patterns remain unspoken, they embed deeply into our familial and personal identities, causing confusion, shame, and needless pain.

The truth is, without clear and honest dialogue, dysfunction becomes a silent family heirloom. Generations carry the weight of unnamed struggles, enduring unnecessary suffering because nobody knew how or had the courage to name it plainly. The silence itself creates cycles of dysfunction, misdiagnosed as curses rather than communication gaps.

Breaking these chains starts with courageous conversations. It requires choosing transparency over comfort, openness over avoidance. Clearly articulating the struggles our families have quietly endured can transform these secret burdens into stepping stones toward healing. Consider these examples:

> "Baby, don't touch alcohol. It destroyed your grandfather's life and your uncle's marriage, and it nearly broke mine too. Our family carries a vulnerability to addiction."
>
> "You know that panic you feel? Grandma wrestled with the same thing, but she never had words like 'anxiety' or 'panic disorder' to describe it. She just called it 'nerves' and suffered silently."
>
> "Your tendency to withdraw? It comes from a lineage of people who handled pain by isolating. It wasn't strength—it was survival."

By naming these pains out loud, we strip away their mysterious power and replace fear with clarity, dysfunction with understanding, and silence with profound healing conversations.

THE DATA DOESN'T LIE

Regularly, headlines announce stark reminders of silence's devastating effects:

"Pastor Resigns over Moral Failure Involving Sexual Misconduct"
"Influential Church Leader Steps Down amid Financial Impropriety"
"Prominent Public Figure Caught in an Addiction Relapse"
"Celebrity Pastor Accused of Abusive Behavior Behind Closed Doors"
"Ministry Leader Admits to Secret Struggles with Substance Abuse"
"High-Profile Religious Leader Reveals Hidden Emotional Affair"
"Youth Pastor Caught in a Sex Sting Operation"

Though the details vary, one devastating truth remains constant: The root cause is always silence.

In every headline-grabbing fall, behind every public breakdown, stands the quiet culprit of unspoken truth. Early on, these leaders and individuals had opportunities to speak clearly about their struggles but chose to remain silent. When dysfunction was small and manageable, they hid it. They did not name it plainly—they didn't say, "I'm struggling with temptation," or "I'm battling addiction," or "I need help." Instead, they isolated in shame and fear.

Over years of pastoral care, ministry experience, and personal transparency, I've collected empirical evidence that all moral failures—whether defined as "missing the mark" (sin), "intentionally crossing boundaries" (transgression), or "engaging in deeply embedded harmful behaviors" (iniquity)—stem from a failure to openly communicate. People stop talking, stop confessing, stop seeking help, and, in that silence, darkness thrives.

Let me break these down real quick: Sin happens when we miss God's intended mark for our lives, many times due to unaddressed pain or temptation left in isolation. This is unintentional. It is not planned. We aimed, but we missed. We've all missed the mark, or fallen short, according to Romans 3:23. Transgression occurs when we knowingly cross lines we previously upheld, usually because accountability has vanished. This is absolutely intentional. It's the equivalent of seeing a sign that reads "No Trespassing" and trespassing anyway. That is transgression. Iniquity is embedded wrongdoing—a moral twisting that happens gradually when secrets become deeply entrenched, deforming our character. Iniquity is making a habit out of trespassing to the point that it becomes a lifestyle. Each of these spiritual failures thrives in silence.

But what if we chose another way? What if clear, consistent confession became our norm? What if transparent dialogue became our default? Preemptive honesty could intercept dysfunction long before it erupts publicly. Early intervention through confession preserves integrity, restores trust, and builds health within communities, ministries, and families. Empirical evidence and lived experience prove this: When we speak honestly, courageously, and openly about our struggles, we halt destructive cycles, protect our communities, and foster genuine, transformative healing.

BREAKING PATTERNS BY SPEAKING

I refuse to be an unspoken-prayer requester.

If I notice an unexpected attraction to another woman, I immediately tell God; my wife, Juliette; and trusted friends. Married doesn't mean dead, but transparency is key to staying spiritually and emotionally alive. Why do I do this?

Because I crave clarity and accountability. Because Juliette's trust matters deeply to me. Because my community needs to see my humanity—not as a weakness but as authenticity that fosters powerful prayer support.

But breaking patterns isn't limited to attraction. Following are a few more examples of what breaking these harmful cycles by speaking out might look like in real, practical scenarios.

If you're wrestling with loneliness, don't quietly spiral into isolation. Reach out intentionally, confessing your need for companionship to a trusted friend or family member. Admit: "I'm struggling with feeling alone. Can we spend some time together soon?" Vulnerability often bridges the gap between isolation and community.

If fear grips your heart—fear of failure, fear of rejection, fear of the unknown—verbalize it clearly to those who care. Admit specifically: "I'm terrified of failing at this new job," or "I'm deeply afraid of rejection in this relationship." Naming the fear directly helps others pray effectively and empowers you to confront it head-on.

If unresolved anger threatens your peace, don't silently harbor bitterness. Speak up, calmly and specifically: "I've been holding on to anger about something you said, and it's affecting my peace. Can we talk about it openly?" Honesty defuses anger and fosters reconciliation.

If persistent feelings of inadequacy or insecurity plague you, acknowledge these emotions openly with someone safe: "I'm struggling with feeling like I'm not enough. I need encouragement and perspective." When you openly discuss insecurity, it loses power and allows supportive truth to be spoken into your life.

Each act of clear confession dismantles destructive cycles. By openly naming struggles, you pave the way for emotional health, authentic relationships, and spiritual growth. Patterns break when we bravely voice our truths.

FROM SURVIVING TO THRIVING IN THIS CULTURE

We inhabit a culture saturated with performance anxiety, driven by triggers, numbed by instant gratification, and relentlessly pressured to maintain superficial appearances. Here, honesty feels revolutionary—even risky.

Yet honesty remains our most reliable path to peace.

Peace doesn't flood our lives simply because we have worship playlists on repeat or scriptures displayed throughout our homes. These practices help, but they aren't transformative in and of themselves.

Peace blossoms when we bravely share our authentic truths, openly and consistently. It thrives when we stop pretending, stop performing, and stop projecting curated perfection. Instead, we embrace vulnerability, choosing authenticity even when our voices shake.

When honesty becomes our lifestyle, we not only survive our performance-driven, trauma-triggered, gratification-saturated culture—we thrive within it. Thriving means experiencing deeper relationships, stronger communities, and clearer emotional health. Thriving means stepping out of the shadows of shame, breaking generational chains, and establishing new legacies of transparency and healing.

In an authentic, honest life, peace doesn't merely visit—it stays, sustained by truth, supported by community, and strengthened by ongoing vulnerability. Honesty creates a life not just worth surviving but worth richly living.

REFLECTION QUESTIONS

1. Have I mistaken silence for strength?
2. What generational dysfunction could shift through honest speech?
3. What am I hiding because of fear or shame?
4. How would clarity change my prayers?
5. Whom can I safely call today and simply ask to listen?

PART 2

RECOVERY 101

11

HOW DO I START TALKING WHEN IT FEELS IMPOSSIBLE?

When silence has been your companion for years, finding your voice again can feel daunting—almost impossible. I deeply identify with the heaviness of unspoken pain because I've lived it. I carried the silence of my sexual abuse trauma for eleven long years. I vividly remember the first time I spoke the truth aloud to my mother—my voice trembling, my heart pounding, and my body filled with fear. Breaking that silence felt impossible, but it was also the beginning of my healing journey.

Learning to speak up wasn't a one-time event. It was a practice, something I had to choose repeatedly. When I married Juliette, it meant confessing to her the addiction I had been wrestling with. It meant staying open in every season—when temptation resurfaced or when relapse occurred. Each confession, each spoken truth gradually made honesty my new normal, teaching me the strength and freedom found only in transparency.

If your story feels locked away, untouched, unnamed, I see you. I've been there. The first step might feel overwhelming, but take heart—you are not alone.

STEP 1: WRITE IT DOWN

The power of written words is immense. When you commit your thoughts, feelings, and pain to paper, something extraordinary happens. Start small—grab paper, a journal, even the back of a receipt. Writing shifts your internal chaos from intangible to tangible, giving you something concrete to hold, see, and manage.

Writing doesn't have to be poetic or polished. Authenticity is what matters most. Write exactly what hurts, what haunts your dreams, and the secrets you've locked away for too long. Words written are truths acknowledged, fears confronted, and secrets unearthed.

Consider it an act of courage—an act just for you. No one else needs to see these words unless you choose to share them. You could even burn them afterward; the important part is the act itself, allowing the reality within to finally be acknowledged.

STEP 2: READ IT OUT LOUD

Now take those words and speak them aloud, into the solitude of an empty room. Allow your voice to break the silence you've maintained.

Hearing your voice express your pain is powerful and healing.

Neuroscience supports this, highlighting how vocalizing trauma can significantly impact your brain. When we speak our truths, our brains begin integrating fragmented traumatic experiences, promoting emotional regulation and clarity.[1]

Your body needs this audible confirmation. The words you speak out loud reinforce a crucial message to your nervous system: "We are safe enough to acknowledge and confront this." Saying your truths aloud dismantles the internal chaos, creating structure and paving the way for deeper emotional healing.

STEP 3: SAY IT TO SOMEONE SAFE

Sharing your truth with another person can feel daunting, but it's a necessary step toward healing. You don't have to broadcast your struggles to everyone—just one safe, trustworthy individual who can hold your story with compassion and care.

Choosing someone safe isn't about perfection. It's about that person's presence, empathy, and willingness to support you without judgment. When you're ready, speak openly and honestly:

> "I'm exhausted from pretending."
> "I'm struggling deeply. I need help."
> "Underneath my anger is profound fear."
> "I'm lonely even when I'm surrounded by people."
> "I've carried shame for too long, and I need to release it."
> "I'm scared that if you know the real me, you'll leave."

Healing is ignited through this act of bravery. Speaking your truth transforms isolation into community, dissolves shame, and invites acceptance and understanding from others.

YOU'RE NOT ALONE; YOU'RE COURAGEOUS

Remember Frank Sheeran from *The Irishman*? He confessed his darkest secrets on his deathbed. Whether his confessions were fully true or not isn't the point—the tragedy lies in the fact that he waited too long to unburden himself.

Some people pride themselves on their ability to keep secrets. And let's be clear: I'm not talking about keeping another person's trust or safeguarding a friend's confidence—those are acts of honor, stewardship, and integrity. I'm talking about the toxic pride that comes from holding on to secrets that should never remain hidden. Secrets that become emotional prisons, silent graveyards where your joy, peace, and relationships go to die.

You know the mindset: "I can handle it myself," or "I don't trust people, so I'll keep this locked up tight." But here's the reality—keeping toxic secrets isn't strength; it's imprisonment. It isn't independence; it's isolation. Secrets eat away at your spirit, corrode your emotional health, and prevent genuine healing and growth. You were never designed to carry these secrets alone. You're not built for solitary confinement in your pain. God created us for connection, community, and openness. Unburdening your secrets doesn't diminish your strength—it unleashes your freedom.

But many silently manage symptoms, numbing themselves or distracting themselves, instead of courageously pursuing true healing or going the extra step to seek therapy. Only about 23 percent of adults in America seek therapy.[2] The actual number might be even lower, because facing our deepest pain head-on is incredibly challenging. And healing isn't linear. It's a messy, unpredictable process filled with breakthroughs and setbacks. It involves facing wounds we've spent years or even decades avoiding.

Don't let your story mirror Frank Sheeran's—waiting until the very end to release the emotional and spiritual weight you've carried. Some secrets don't deserve the power they hold. It's time to speak, to release, to find freedom long before the end of your days.

If you've started confronting your pain, you might feel isolated, like something's inherently wrong with you. Let me reassure you right now: Nothing is wrong with you. In fact, your willingness to confront your pain head-on proves your immense bravery. I recently spoke with a man from Germany who felt discouraged about his progress. But even his decision to reach out for support was a monumental step forward. Every brave choice matters, every honest acknowledgment of pain is progress, and each step counts profoundly in your journey toward healing.

Remember the lepers from Scripture? They were forced to live on the outskirts of towns, isolated and misunderstood, and required to shout "Unclean!" whenever someone else approached (Lev. 13:45). Their very presence was stigmatized, and their condition was seen as permanent and shameful. Imagine the courage it took for one of them to break from his isolation, step into public view, and boldly ask for healing. In doing so, he risked ridicule, rejection, even further ostracism, but it was the only path toward freedom and wholeness.

Starting your healing journey might feel just as risky, frightening, and isolating. You might feel like everyone else around you has their lives together and you're the only one struggling. But you're also one of the courageous few willing to confront truth, challenge silence, and step boldly toward healing—and perhaps even start therapy. Your bravery not only transforms your life but inspires others to seek freedom as well.

THERAPY IS RECOVERY, NOT SURGERY

There's a common misconception about therapy—that it's something you seek only after you've completely crashed, burned out, or hit rock bottom. While therapy can certainly help stabilize you after a crisis, the deeper, more powerful work is in the recovery that follows. Think of it like physical therapy after surgery. During surgery, you're unconscious—you don't feel the procedure. The real challenge and growth begin afterward, in rehabilitation, when you're fully awake, conscious, and working intentionally to heal.

Recovery, or emotional rehabilitation, often involves confronting pain head-on. It's about addressing core wounds and trauma directly and working through them, rather than merely stabilizing symptoms. This part of the journey can feel more intense, painful, and exhausting precisely because you're awake, aware, and actively participating in your healing. You're rebuilding emotional strength, resilience, and health from the inside out, and that process requires persistence and courage.

This is especially important to grasp if your trauma occurred long ago. If something happened when you were five and now you're thirty, healing won't happen overnight. It's a journey, not an event. It takes time, patience, and sometimes more sessions than you anticipated. Recovery is rarely linear—there will be highs and lows, moments of profound breakthrough, and periods of feeling stuck or overwhelmed.

Yet despite the discomfort, unpredictability, and awkwardness, recovery through therapy is incredibly worthwhile. It's about reclaiming your true self, building resilience to handle life's inevitable stressors, and learning healthier ways to respond when old patterns and triggers surface. It's a process of empowerment, giving you the tools and understanding needed to create lasting, meaningful change in your life. Your investment in recovery is an investment in freedom, peace, and emotional health.

PAUL'S THORN, JESUS'S GRACE

Years ago I experienced a life-changing revelation from 2 Corinthians 12, where Paul described a persistent thorn in his flesh. Paul begged God—not once but three times—to remove this source of continual pain. And here's the remarkable thing: Jesus Himself responded to Paul, saying, "My grace is sufficient for you, for My strength is made perfect in weakness" (v. 9).

Why was it Jesus who answered Paul? Because He uniquely understood Paul's experience. In the garden of Gethsemane, Jesus also pleaded three times for relief, asking God to take away His own "cup of suffering" (Matt. 26:39 NLT). Yet, unlike Paul, Jesus heard only silence. He willingly drank from that cup, endured the pain, and completed His mission. Jesus provided Paul with the very answer He Himself never received: the assurance that grace was sufficient even when pain lingered.

Here's the truth I want deeply ingrained in your heart: Some wounds, some scars, some pains never completely disappear. They heal over but leave behind reminders—sometimes subtle, sometimes sharp. Think of someone who underwent a painful surgery and now feels a familiar ache every time the winter cold sets in. The drop in temperature isn't causing new damage; it's merely reminding them of a past trauma. The wound is healed, but the memory remains, often triggered by certain conditions or environments.

Our emotional and spiritual wounds can operate in the same way. You might be healed in many areas, but certain situations, seasons, or environments can trigger the old ache. It doesn't mean you're not healed—it means you're human. And in those moments God's grace steps in powerfully, providing strength, comfort, and resilience. His grace doesn't always eliminate every trace of pain, but it sustains us in it, reminding us that in our weakest moments His strength shines brightest.

FROM SURVIVING TO THRIVING

Too often we settle for survival, trapped in a mentality shaped by trauma, pain, or disappointment. We comfort ourselves with statements such as these:

"At least I made it through."

"It could've been worse."

"God carried me through it."

These statements, while truthful, can inadvertently become ceilings that limit our growth. It's almost as if we're suggesting that God brought us through our pain only to drop us off at a place where we simply survive, barely getting by without flourishing.

But here's the truth: Survival isn't the fullness of God's story for you. He didn't bring you through your darkest valleys just so you could spend the rest of your life walking with a limp emotionally, relationally, or spiritually. God intends more for you—He intends for you to thrive.

This book is for the brave souls who refuse to settle for a mediocre, survival-mode existence. It's for those who want not only to heal but to reclaim and surpass their previous capabilities. Imagine someone who tore his Achilles tendon playing basketball. Yes, he survived the injury, but thriving means he undergoes the hard, often painful work of rehabilitation. Thriving means he's not just back on the court; he's playing better than ever, even after the injury.

Similarly, maybe you've never been able to deeply connect or genuinely love because of past emotional or physical trauma. The journey from surviving to thriving means courageously doing the necessary emotional work to heal. It means stepping into relationships that are richer, deeper, and more fulfilling than you ever dreamed possible. You're able to love and connect in ways previously inaccessible to you.

Thriving is about reclaiming your story—not just enduring your past but transcending it. It's about experiencing abundant life, purposeful joy, and meaningful relationships. This journey takes commitment, vulnerability, and perseverance, but the life waiting on the other side is worth every step you take to get there.

WHAT RECOVERY LOOKS LIKE

Recovery isn't just getting by; it's actively building a life in which trauma no longer dictates your responses. True recovery means that when triggered, you respond thoughtfully instead of reacting impulsively, and when old patterns surface, you recognize them immediately and consciously choose a healthier path.

- You say confidently, "That was my old story—this is my new one."
- You feel safe enough to trust again after experiencing betrayal or emotional abuse.
- You set clear, healthy boundaries without guilt or fear of abandonment.
- You recognize your worth and affirm yourself even after enduring verbal or emotional abuse.
- You pursue meaningful relationships without fear of repeating past relational trauma.
- You practice self-care consistently, knowing you are worthy of rest and compassion after years of neglect.
- You speak up calmly and assertively in situations where you previously felt powerless.
- You embrace vulnerability, allowing others to see and know your authentic self without shame.
- You express your emotions freely, knowing they won't overwhelm or consume you.
- You cultivate a spirituality that feels safe, genuine, and nurturing, especially after experiencing spiritual abuse.

Remember, recovery is a courageous and ongoing journey. Each step forward, no matter how small it feels, is progress worth celebrating. You're not merely surviving; you're building a beautiful, resilient life beyond your trauma.

THREE ESSENTIAL TRUTHS

Let's spin the block and emphasize this again clearly, deeply, and unmistakably:

TRUTH 1: YOU EXPERIENCED TRAUMA. Your story, your pain, your wounds—these are valid. They happened, and acknowledging them is vital.

TRUTH 2: YOU SURVIVED. You made it through. Even if you feel battered and worn, you're still here—breathing, living proof of strength and resilience.

TRUTH 3: YOU ARE MEANT TO THRIVE. Survival isn't the end goal; it's merely the starting line. You weren't pulled from life's turbulent waters just to lie on the shore, barely breathing as waves occasionally wash over you. You were pulled to safety to live, grow, flourish, and thrive fully.

Let this third truth deeply resonate and guide your journey—not just for this moment, but for the lifetime ahead. Your purpose isn't just to endure but to genuinely thrive.

In the chapters ahead, we'll walk toward that goal of deep and lasting recovery on a trauma-informed path, drawing wisdom from trusted experts such as Janina Fisher and Dr. Bessel van der Kolk, integrated with spiritual insights, scriptural truths, and the strength of a supportive community.

You were never meant to walk this path alone.

Real, abundant life begins now.

REFLECTION QUESTIONS

1. Does therapy scare me?
2. What past experiences shape my views about therapy?
3. Am I open to trying therapy?
4. What resources do I have to help find a therapist?
5. What would thriving—not just surviving—look like in my life?

STAGE 1

SAFETY AND STABILIZATION

As a first step, you must first learn to comprehend the effects of trauma: to recognize common symptoms and to understand the meaning of overwhelming body sensations, intrusive emotions, and distorted cognitive schemas. The achievement of safety and stability rests on the following tasks:

- Establishing bodily safety: e.g., abstinence from self-injury.
- Establishment of a safe environment: e.g., a secure living situation, non-abusive relationships, a job and/or regular income, adequate supports.
- Establishment of emotional stability: e.g., ability to calm the body, regulate impulses, self-soothe, manage post-traumatic symptoms triggered by mundane events.

—*Janina Fisher*[1]

12

SAFE BODY

Janina Fisher outlines the first stage of trauma recovery with powerful clarity: safety and stabilization. And the very first place that needs to become safe isn't your relationships, your job, or even your home—it's your body.

Your body must first become safe from you.

Sit with that for a moment. Let's slow it down and really get this. Why does your body need to be safe *from* you first? Because trauma messes you up on the inside—it tricks you into becoming your own worst enemy. Imagine being so hurt that you start believing you deserve it, and without realizing it, you start doing to yourself what others once did to you. You might starve your body, feed it junk, ignore your own tiredness, push past your limits, or punish yourself in subtle ways.

Until we see our bodies as valuable and worthy of love, care, and respect—as precious creations that deserve protection—real and lasting safety will stay out of reach. You gotta make peace with you first, right where you are.

This isn't about diets or fitness. It's a dignity question.

Is my body a safe home for me?
Do I nourish my body, or do I punish it?
Do I listen when it speaks or silence it with distractions?
Am I gentle when overwhelmed, or do I shame myself for feeling?

Take a moment here. Seriously. Stop reading. Set a timer for five minutes. Let the Holy Spirit guide your reflection. What's the truth about how you really treat your body?

SAFETY BEGINS IN THE FLESH

Many of us carry trauma quietly, secretly, using coping mechanisms that often cause us harm:

Numbing emotions with food
Endless scrolling through social media
Seeking escape through sex or substances
Overworking to avoid facing our feelings
Consistently neglecting rest or adequate sleep
Avoiding medical care or basic self-care routines
Engaging in negative self-talk or self-criticism

The issue isn't having coping mechanisms—we all need ways to deal with pain. The real problem is when our coping methods silently start working against us. Imagine these habits like termites hidden deep within the walls of a house—on the outside everything looks fine, but inside they're quietly causing serious damage. Over time these hidden coping strategies chip away at our sense of dignity and self-worth, leaving us hollow and disconnected, questioning our value. It's crucial to recognize and address these harmful habits before they undermine the very foundation of who we are.

When our bodies don't feel safe, everything else destabilizes. Emotions spill uncontrollably, reactions become extreme, memory suffers, and sleep deteriorates. We lose sight of what grounding even feels like. So we need to be purposeful in creating a sense of safety for our bodies.

Creating bodily safety involves intentional acts:

Slowing down when anxious
Eating nourishing foods
Walking mindfully to ground and center
Connecting deeply with trusted people
Resting without guilt

Your body is your home. Treating it kindly isn't optional—it's essential.

POLYVAGAL THEORY: A ROAD MAP TO SAFETY

Polyvagal theory explains that our bodies have three main states:

1. **FIGHT OR FLIGHT:** Feeling threatened, scared, or defensive—your heart races, and you feel anxious or angry.
2. **SHUTDOWN:** Feeling numb, disconnected, hopeless—you are emotionally and physically withdrawn.
3. **SAFETY:** Feeling calm, secure, and connected—you are able to engage with life confidently and warmly.

Healing from trauma isn't about always feeling great. In fact, trauma recovery often feels uncomfortable, confusing, or even painful at times. A crucial part of healing is becoming self-aware enough to notice when your body and emotions start signaling that something isn't right. Maybe you feel your heart racing, tension rising in your chest, or a numbness creeping in. Perhaps you find yourself quickly irritated or retreating inward, shutting down from those around you. These signs indicate that you're becoming dysregulated.

The key is not to beat yourself up or push through these feelings but rather to gently acknowledge them as signals guiding you back to safety. When I learned to recognize these cues, everything shifted. Instead of chasing highs or numbing lows, I practiced returning to safety by taking deep, mindful breaths (you can catch me on *The Basement* doing this almost every episode), grounding myself in the truth of Scripture, or engaging my senses—feeling textures, noticing sounds and smells around me.

SAFE FROM OTHERS—AND MYSELF

It's easier to spot unsafe people than it is to admit we are unsafe toward ourselves. I know folks who would never tolerate someone else harming them. Yet they will

binge eat their grief,
drink through loneliness,
scroll endlessly through anxiety,
numb pain through sex or substances,
overwork to exhaustion,
isolate themselves in depression, or
allow chronic stress without rest or relief.

I've been there myself. This isn't coping—it's socially acceptable self-harm. But let's unpack when coping crosses over into sabotage. Coping becomes sabotage when the methods you use to momentarily relieve pain or discomfort start creating additional issues. It's subtle at first—you convince yourself you're just taking the edge off or unwinding from stress. But gradually these habits take control, demanding more of your time, energy, and health.

Consider the following examples of when coping crosses into sabotage.

The solution creates new problems: One drink to unwind turns into nightly drinking that affects your sleep and relationships.

Temporary relief turns habitual: Comfort food becomes a constant companion, negatively affecting your physical health.

Your coping method isolates you: Endless scrolling or binge-watching pulls you away from meaningful interactions, deepening loneliness.

You neglect your basic needs: Overworking becomes an escape, causing exhaustion and burnout.

Recognize that this isn't about shame—it's about clarity and honesty. This awareness is your powerful first step toward stabilization and care. Your body needs—and deserves—this healing.

HEALING THE BODY TO RESTORE THE SOUL

Let me make this clear.

You can't binge and fully heal.

You can't numb out and expect regulation.

You can't starve your body and see your heart flourish.

You can't neglect rest and achieve emotional stability.

You can't consistently override your body's signals and remain emotionally healthy.

Your body holds your trauma—and it's precisely where healing must begin. Imagine trauma as emotional and physical memories stored deep within the muscles, nerves, and tissues. Your body remembers even when your mind tries to forget. Healing that trauma isn't simply about talking through your pain or reshaping your thoughts—though those things matter—it's about nurturing and reestablishing safety within your physical being.

When I shifted from viewing my body with judgment or resentment to treating it with reverence, patience, and compassionate care, everything changed profoundly. This approach allowed the stored trauma to gently surface, be acknowledged, and ultimately be released, transforming how I felt, moved, and interacted with the world. This led to improved sleep quality, enhanced clarity of mind, transformed cravings, increased energy and vitality, and stabler emotions and reactions.

We're not looking for perfection here but consistent safety and care.

SCRIPTURE AS A REGULATORY ANCHOR

Let me give you one more strategy to help bring your body back into a place of safety when dysregulation hits: using Scripture as an anchor. Scripture isn't just comforting poetry—it's a grounding wire.

Take Psalm 69, for example. The whole passage sounds like a therapy session: "Let not the floodwater overflow me. . . . I am in trouble; hear me speedily. Draw near to my soul, and redeem it; deliver me" (vv. 15, 17–18). This scripture captures the voice of someone deeply dysregulated—someone feeling overwhelmed, begging not simply for rescue but for calm, for grounding, for regulation. David, the writer, called on God to help him in the middle of a hard situation, just as we need to learn to do when our bodies show signs of being triggered. When you start noticing a stress response, you need Scripture to stand on—not just motivational quotes.

Here are a few more powerful verses that offer stabilization:

- Psalm 16:9: "Therefore my heart is glad, and my glory rejoices; my flesh also will rest in hope."
- Proverbs 14:30: "A peaceful heart leads to a healthy body" (NLT).
- Psalm 4:8: "In peace I will lie down and sleep, for you alone, O LORD, will keep me safe" (NLT).
- Isaiah 26:3: "You will keep in perfect peace all who trust in you, all whose thoughts are fixed on you" (NLT).
- Philippians 4:7: "And the peace of God, which surpasses all understanding, will guard your hearts and minds through Christ Jesus."

Reminding ourselves of these scriptures won't act as instant magic, but it will help us make steady, faithful progress toward peace. And when our hearts and minds are at peace, our whole bodies will come into alignment with God. Think of Scripture as a powerful anchor for your soul. The bigger the ship, the heavier the anchor it needs to stay grounded in turbulent waters.

Did you know ancient anchors were often just heavy stones tied to ropes? Modern anchors are specifically engineered to dig into the seabed and grip tighter as the ship pulls against them. Even in a storm, a well-anchored ship might sway, but it won't drift away. Your soul works the same way. The heavier your struggles, traumas, or challenges, the stronger and deeper your anchor needs to be.

Scripture isn't just nice words—it digs deep into the bedrock of truth, grounding you firmly. You may sway emotionally during storms, but you won't drift away, because your soul is anchored in something immovable and eternal. That's the power of anchoring your mind and heart in God's Word—it holds you steady when everything else feels shaky.

If you find yourself in a dysregulated moment when you feel overwhelmed just thinking about finding the right scripture to ground you, I would point you toward the Psalms. They are especially powerful grounding tools. Much like how an herbalist carefully selects leaves and herbs and blends their medicinal properties to heal the body, the Psalms blend powerful spiritual truths to heal the soul. The book of Psalms, notably the largest book in the Bible with the longest chapter (Ps. 119) and one of the shortest chapters (Ps. 117), uniquely addresses the full spectrum of human emotions and experiences.

Think of the Psalms as a collection of carefully selected leaves, each with unique spiritual properties—comfort, reassurance, courage, peace, strength—brought together to provide holistic healing and emotional regulation. Here are five examples to ground you when dysregulation approaches:

1. Psalm 69:17–18: "Hear me speedily. Draw near to my soul."
2. Psalm 46:1: "God is our refuge and strength, a very present help in trouble."
3. Psalm 23:4: "Even when I walk through the darkest valley, I will not be afraid" (NLT).
4. Psalm 34:4: "I sought the LORD, and He heard me, and delivered me from all my fears."
5. Psalm 91:2: "He is my refuge and my fortress; my God, in Him I will trust."

Scripture becomes somatic, deeply felt, and profoundly stabilizing. This is where healing begins—this is how your body and soul become anchored and safe again.

REFLECTION QUESTIONS

1. How do I treat my body when I feel triggered?
2. Do I gently soothe my body or punish it harshly?
3. Is my body safe from external harm? Is it safe from me?
4. Do I need a social media pause for genuine healing?
5. What's one habit I can adjust today toward safety and stability?

13

SAFE ZONE

If my body is the first place trauma takes root, then my environment is the soil that either supports my healing or stunts it. I need a safe body, yes, but equally important is having a safe zone—a physical, emotional, and spiritual environment that lets me breathe deeply, without worry or vigilance.

Think about planting a seed: No matter how healthy the seed is, it can't grow if the soil is toxic or lacks nutrients. Similarly, no matter how much internal healing you pursue, your progress will be limited if your external surroundings remain chaotic or triggering. Your safe zone is your sanctuary, a space intentionally crafted to restore, refresh, and rejuvenate you. It's a place that protects your peace, supports your progress, and honors your healing journey.

When you don't have a safe zone, it can be easy to step back into a chaotic environment and quickly undo progress and reactivate trauma responses. Your body remembers even the smallest details of past harm, down to the scent in the air or the tone of a familiar voice. It recalls moments your mind may try desperately to forget. Healing demands that you acknowledge this reality: No level of internal stability can fully hold without a genuinely safe external environment. You must actively protect your healing by ensuring the spaces you inhabit support rather than undermine your hard-earned progress.

Imagine trying to heal a burn while standing next to a blazing fire. You might soothe it briefly, but the heat constantly threatens to reopen the wound, keeping the pain fresh and ongoing. That's exactly how it feels to regulate your nervous system in environments that continually unsettle or provoke you.

Triggers aren't imaginary—they embed themselves deeply into your senses. They exist in the subtle sounds of footsteps, the familiar scent of a room, the texture of a blanket, the sight of particular faces, or the rhythm of daily routines. Your body holds on to these sensory memories vividly, remembering exactly where it was, what it felt like, and how intensely it reacted during traumatic moments. To support your healing, your environment must gently reassure your nervous system that it's finally safe to let down its guard.

WHAT IS A SAFE ZONE?

So what exactly does this sense of safety that we've been talking about look like? Scripture lays a clear foundation: "In peace I will lie down and sleep, for you alone, O Lord, will keep me safe" (Ps. 4:8 NLT).

True safety transcends locked doors or soundproof rooms—it's deeply rooted in presence, in who or what fills the space around you. It's about feeling emotionally secure enough to exhale fully, knowing that your surroundings and the people near you foster healing rather than harm. Safety is found in environments filled with compassion, understanding, and stability, places where trust is reinforced rather than eroded. It's the difference between feeling constantly on guard and experiencing genuine rest, between anticipating threats and welcoming peace. Safety nurtures and sustains you, allowing your heart and nervous system the freedom to heal fully and authentically.

Psalm 18:48 states, "You hold me safe beyond the reach of my enemies" (NLT). Safety means I'm no longer trapped in a perpetual state of fight, flight, freeze, or fawn. It's stepping out of constant alertness, vigilance, or emotional numbness into a space where my nervous system can relax and recuperate. It means recognizing when my body is bracing against threats—even imagined ones—and consciously choosing environments and people that reassure my inner self that it's finally safe to release tension. Safety is experiencing the profound relief of resting deeply, without anticipating the next threat or crisis. It is reclaiming peace, moment by moment, and giving my body and mind the nurturing space they need to heal fully.

REDESIGN YOUR LIFE FOR PEACE

As you're considering cultivating this sense of safety, you'll want to think about it in multiple layers:

your personal space
the lighting around you
your neighborhood
your media intake
your social media feeds
your friendships and relationships

All of these layers matter because your environment directly influences your emotional well-being, mental clarity, and physical health. Your personal space can either promote relaxation or amplify anxiety, depending on how cluttered or peaceful it feels. Lighting around you can soothe your nervous system or overstimulate it. The degree of safety in your neighborhood can enhance your sense of security or leave you in constant alertness. Media intake, including news and entertainment, shapes your mood, worldview, and emotional resilience. Social media feeds influence your self-esteem, comparison tendencies, and overall emotional stability. Friendships and relationships either provide healing connections or reinforce trauma patterns.

Each layer interacts with your nervous system, either nourishing or depleting your emotional reserves. Recognizing and optimizing these layers is crucial in crafting an environment supportive of your healing journey.

Remember, safe zones don't happen accidentally—they are intentionally designed. So here are a few things you can do as you design your safe zone, layer by layer:

- Rearrange your living spaces for comfort.
- Invest in noise-canceling headphones.
- Adjust lighting to soothe your senses.
- Unfollow sources of digital chaos.
- Mute notifications from apps or platforms that frequently stress or distract you.
- Limit the amount of time spent browsing emotionally draining websites or forums.
- Unsubscribe from email newsletters or groups that don't align with your current journey toward peace.

Safe zones don't just appear—they are carefully crafted to align with your unique emotional, mental, and spiritual needs. You consciously select who and what enter your space, deliberately choosing calming environments, and actively removing influences that unsettle or disrupt your peace. It's an ongoing process of refinement, a continual assessment of what brings comfort and what detracts from your stability.

Remember, you don't owe everyone—or every situation—unlimited access to your peace.

GOD DIDN'T DO THAT TO YOU

Sometimes we confuse the unsafe environments that come from life's natural consequences with divine punishment, especially if we've been taught to see God primarily as a stern Judge rather than a loving Father. Many of us grew up hearing messages that portrayed God as constantly waiting to punish us for mistakes, reinforcing the belief that every hardship or consequence was His direct retaliation. Our understanding of God deeply influences our response to life's outcomes—whether we perceive them as punishments or as natural consequences of our actions.

I vividly remember sitting in my office one afternoon when a young man from my ministry came in visibly shaken and emotionally burdened. He had been part of my young-adult group, and I had walked closely with him, witnessing his ongoing struggles. As he sat down, eyes filled with tears, he shared that he had contracted HIV after years of promiscuity. His pain was palpable, and as he spoke, his tears triggered my own. We sat silently, the weight of his revelation filling the room.

Then he said something that troubled me: "I don't know why God chose me to go through this, but not my will but Thine be done." His words felt like a heavy blow—not because he was turning to God, but because his perception was so distorted. In that moment I had to gently yet firmly correct his narrative. "God didn't do this to you. He's not that kind of Father."

God offers boundaries, not punishments—guidelines designed

not to stifle joy but to protect it. These boundaries, clearly outlined in both the Old and New Testaments, aren't there to limit us arbitrarily; they're markers that preserve the beauty and depth of our relationships with God and with others. When I explained this to my friend, I shared an example from my own life.

I love my sons. If they want to play outside, I gladly encourage them, yet I set clear boundaries: "You can play in the front yard, but don't run into the street." These boundaries are meant not to restrict their fun but to ensure their safety. If they choose to ignore these boundaries and, God forbid, end up hurt or scared by running into the street, that wouldn't be me causing them harm. The harm arises naturally from their disregarding the protective boundary. Similarly, the consequences we face from our choices are not punishments from a vengeful God—they're simply the natural results of our stepping beyond the wise and loving boundaries He set to safeguard us.

Unsafe environments can emerge from our unsafe choices—but that's not always the case. Sometimes unsafe environments result from the harmful actions and brokenness of others. Abuse, trauma, and emotional damage frequently come from someone else's choices, reflecting their own unresolved pain or flaws. It's crucial to recognize this distinction clearly: Whether from our choices or those of others, these environments and their consequences aren't divine punishment but human realities requiring compassionate care and healing.

So rather than assume that our current unsafe circumstances are God's doing, let's take a moment to reflect on what's actually happening. Let's take a note from the practical wisdom in Proverbs 3:21–26: "Don't lose sight of common sense and discernment. Hang on to them. . . . They keep you safe. . . . You will lie down and sleep soundly. . . . The Lord is your security" (NLT).

This is your blueprint for creating a safe zone:

- **DISCERNMENT:** Reflect on what's really going on and whether your unsafe environment is a result of choices you've made or choices others have made.
- **HEALTHY BOUNDARIES:** Take the reality you've discerned and set guidelines for what you need for a safe body and a safe zone. As you encounter experiences and people, hold them up to these guidelines to determine whether they contribute to a safe zone for you. If not, they are not for you and your new mental health. Protect your boundaries and keep your zone safe.
- **RESTFUL SLEEP:** Prioritize consistent, restorative sleep as a nonnegotiable part of your healing. Sleep is where your nervous system downshifts, your body repairs itself, and your brain processes unresolved stress and trauma. An unsafe life produces restless nights; a safe zone protects your right to rest. Creating rhythms, routines, and environments that support deep sleep is not laziness—it's regulation. A well-rested body is far less vulnerable to emotional hijacking and survival-based decision-making.
- **SPIRITUAL TRUST:** Develop a grounded trust that you are not carrying your life alone. Spiritual trust is not denial, avoidance, or blind positivity—it is the settled confidence that God is present, attentive, and trustworthy even when outcomes feel uncertain. This kind of trust allows your nervous system to release hypervigilance and your soul to stop bracing for impact. When you trust God, you no longer have to control everything to feel safe.

Each of us has a unique set of needs, and your safe zone should align with your unique emotional, physical, and spiritual requirements. Choose activities or environments that ground and restore you. Find what works specifically for you—and then work it.

REGULATE YOUR TIMING

Safety isn't just about *where* you are but *when* you are. Timing plays a critical role in emotional regulation. I've discovered that certain times of day, particular situations, or specific emotional states can heighten my vulnerability. Understanding this has been key—I've learned to notice signs of overwhelm early, like increased tension, irritability, or a sense of detachment. Recognizing these cues helps me proactively choose the moments and methods that best restore calm and stability to my nervous system.

Here's a practical example: When I want physical rest, I don't play worship music (I know that sounds crazy to my Christian fam). Worship music almost instantly stirs spiritual emotion and tears in me, which, for me as an empath, doesn't equate to physical rest. Instead, I choose jazz—instrumental, no lyrics, no emotional heavy lifting. Just music that matches my intention.

Here are a few more examples:

If you're emotionally drained after a long day, avoid engaging in heavy or emotional conversations; choose quiet, restful activities like reading or taking a calming walk.

If you're physically exhausted, don't try to push through an intense workout; opt for gentle stretching or meditation to help your body recover.

If you're mentally overwhelmed after work, avoid immediately diving into complex household chores; instead, take a short break to decompress, perhaps listening to nature sounds or practicing deep-breathing exercises.

Even in a safe environment, poor timing can lead to emotional chaos. Consider conversations initiated when you're feeling hungry, exhausted, or lonely. It's not the environment's fault—it's timing.

Make peace with saying, "Now isn't the right time." Return to these conversations when you're regulated.

WHEN ALL ELSE FAILS, CALL HIS NAME

Proverbs 18:10 reassures us that "the name of the Lord is a strong tower; the righteous run to it and are safe."

When your space feels unsafe, when anxiety peaks, or you find yourself spiraling, call His name. Whisper it. Cry it out. Shout it if you must. "Jesus."

His name alone brings peace because He is the Prince of Peace.

And here's the reality: Not everyone has the privilege of immediately changing their physical environment. Maybe your home feels chaotic, your neighborhood is challenging, or you're reading this in a situation like prison where your surroundings feel entirely beyond your control. I've walked with loved ones who've spent significant time in environments they couldn't escape, and I personally know what it's like to live in and survive environmentally traumatizing neighborhoods. But even when external peace seems impossible, true peace can still flourish within.

Proverbs 18:10 promises that His name is your strong tower, and Philippians 4:7 assures us that "the peace of God, which surpasses all understanding, will guard your hearts and minds through Christ Jesus." You may not control every external factor, but you absolutely can cultivate internal peace. When your external environment fails you, let your internal sanctuary be strong. Call His name, and let peace anchor you deep within.

REFLECTION QUESTIONS

1. Is my current space truly safe?
2. What triggers exist in my environment?
3. Are my boundaries strong enough to protect my healing journey?
4. Which relationships, habits, or environments do I need to reconsider?
5. Is it time to redesign my life—both spiritually and physically?

14

SAFE MIND

Once my body is safe and my environment is stable, my mind becomes the critical next frontier of recovery. Because everything flows from there. If my mind isn't regulated—if it's clouded by shame, stuck replaying traumatic memories, or trapped in persistent grief—my healing stalls. My peace is compromised. My body tenses. My relationships become strained. My spirit dims.

Scripture clearly guides us: "Guard your heart above all else, for it determines the course of your life" (Prov. 4:23 NLT).

Guarding your heart isn't about paranoia or constant suspicion—it's far deeper than mere vigilance or fear-driven caution. It's about cultivating intentional stewardship, carefully and deliberately deciding what you allow into your mental and emotional spaces. Just as diligent gardeners are mindful of the soil they use, the seeds they plant, and the weeds they remove, guarding your mind requires you to thoughtfully assess every influence you encounter. This means evaluating the words spoken to you, the images you consume, the company you keep, and even your own internal dialogue.

Consider your mind like a carefully tended garden. Without constant attention, weeds of negativity, bitterness, self-doubt, or destructive thoughts quickly take root and can choke out joy, peace, and emotional health. Intentional stewardship involves regularly pruning these harmful influences—recognizing toxic thoughts or messages when they appear and swiftly removing them before they have the chance to deepen their roots.

It's also about proactively planting and nurturing positive, life-giving thoughts that affirm your worth, purpose, and healing journey. This is not passive work; it's active and ongoing, and it requires vigilance paired with compassion. Your mental garden won't flourish overnight, but through consistent care, attention, and wise regulation, you can cultivate an internal landscape that supports growth, fosters peace, and encourages ongoing renewal. Guarding your heart, therefore, isn't about isolating yourself—it's about creating an environment in your mind where healthy, hopeful, and healing thoughts can thrive.

THE MIND AS THE FOUNDATION

Everything begins in the mind.

If I don't guard my thoughts, my words become careless.

If I don't guard my words, my behaviors deteriorate.

If I don't guard my behaviors, my body acts out destructively.

It's all interconnected. Your thoughts shape your emotional state, your emotional state influences your words, your words manifest in actions, and your actions affect your body and your relationships. When negativity, anxiety, or shame dominates your mind, it spills over into every aspect of your life, creating a ripple effect that disrupts your emotional balance, undermines your self-esteem, and strains your connections with others.

Protecting your mind, therefore, involves intentional, proactive vigilance. It's about actively choosing the thoughts you entertain and the narratives you reinforce. By doing so, you nurture emotional resilience and a stable foundation for your well-being. Just like a weak link in a chain can compromise the entire structure, unchecked negative thoughts can undermine your peace and progress. Conversely, cultivating a healthy mental environment creates a reinforcing cycle of positivity, growth, and peace. This intentional cultivation isn't about ignoring difficulties or avoiding reality; it's about creating an internal space resilient enough to handle challenges without collapsing under their weight.

PEACE ISN'T PASSIVE

Philippians 4:6–9 lays a clear foundation for peace:

> Don't worry about anything.
> Pray about everything.
> Express your needs clearly to God.
> Be grateful for His past interventions.
> Then experience peace.

In this passage, Paul wasn't dismissing anxiety. He was providing practical guidance for moving through it: Prayer is your tool. Gratitude is your posture. Peace is your reward.

Paul's words assure that God's peace "will guard your hearts and minds through Christ Jesus" (v. 7). I've discovered that following Paul's guideline—combining prayer with immediate gratitude—calms internal storms quickly, rewires neural pathways, and reestablishes my access to hope.

It's critical to understand, however, that peace isn't passive—it demands intentional, consistent effort. Achieving peace requires active engagement, persistent practice, and disciplined awareness. Anxiety, fear, and stress don't simply vanish because we wish them away or ignore them. They are confronted and transformed through conscious, repeated action. This active pursuit of peace includes continually bringing our concerns to God, specifically and transparently. It involves deliberately recalling and recounting moments when we've experienced His faithfulness, allowing gratitude to shape our mental landscape.

Practicing peace actively means recognizing and disrupting cycles of worry and replacing them with trust. It means choosing prayer even when our emotions resist it, choosing gratitude even when circumstances challenge it, and choosing trust even when our logic contests it. Peace isn't a passive emotion that merely arrives—it's an active state we intentionally cultivate through repeated choices and disciplined spiritual practice.

Paul went on to instruct us to "fix your thoughts on what is true, and honorable, and right, and pure, and lovely, and admirable" (v. 8 NLT). This is trauma-informed practice in action, and it's essential to understand what "trauma informed" means. Being trauma informed is about recognizing that trauma shapes how we perceive the world, how we interact with others, and how our bodies and brains respond to everyday situations. It means being aware of how past hurts affect our current emotional and psychological states, and it requires us to actively create environments—mentally, emotionally, and physically—that support healing rather than exacerbate wounds.

Paul wasn't instructing us to ignore pain or pretend it doesn't exist. Instead, his words guide us toward intentionally anchoring ourselves in truths that actively promote healing and resilience. When we deliberately fix our thoughts on what's true, honorable, right, pure, lovely, and admirable, we are engaging our brains in a powerful neurological process. Neuroscience confirms that the focus of our attention shapes the neural pathways within our brains—effectively rewiring our cognitive structures.[1] If our attention constantly rests on negative, anxious, or traumatic experiences, our brains strengthen pathways associated with stress, fear, and pessimism.

Conversely, when we intentionally redirect our thoughts to healthy, positive, life-affirming realities, our brains develop stronger pathways for resilience, emotional balance, and positivity. Think of it as mental conditioning. Just as muscles get stronger with regular exercise, the mind grows more resilient and peaceful with the consistent practice of focusing on truths that build you up rather than tear you down.

Practically speaking, it's similar to choosing between driving five minutes to buy junk food or taking an extra twenty minutes to get healthy food. Both options exist. Both choices are available. But one nourishes and strengthens your body, while the other temporarily satisfies but ultimately undermines your health. Similarly, there's plenty of negativity, tragedy, and dysfunction readily available to consume in our world. But there is also abundant beauty, kindness, generosity, and inspiration. Which you choose to focus on will profoundly affect your mental and emotional health, guiding your nervous system toward either greater peace or greater anxiety.

When I'm overwhelmed, my task isn't self-shaming. It's gently redirecting my focus.

HORNINESS ISN'T A SIN

Did you know horniness isn't a sin? I know you're probably thinking, *Tim, where did that come from?*

All right, let's get real real.

When I was a young-adult pastor, most of the people in my ministry were single and wrestling with sexual desire. Let's call it what it is—they were horny. That's not sinful; that's human biology at work. Unfortunately, the church hasn't always handled this reality well. Instead of teaching healthy, biblical truths about sex and sexuality, we've often cloaked these discussions in shame and secrecy, unintentionally creating a culture of suppression and hidden struggles.

We have to acknowledge that purity culture, though well-intentioned, often failed to achieve its purpose. Instead of celebrating sexuality as a beautiful, God-given gift meant for enjoyment within marriage, purity culture frequently communicated the message that sex was inherently dirty, shameful, and taboo—right up until the wedding night. Suddenly what had been "forbidden" was expected to feel normal, beautiful, and free from guilt overnight. This has caused confusion, shame, and anxiety for many, contributing to secretive behaviors, unhealthy relationships with sexuality, and difficulty experiencing genuine intimacy within marriage.

Sexual desire isn't destructive—what becomes destructive is our inability or unwillingness to establish clear, healthy boundaries around it. Having sexual urges simply means your body is functioning exactly as God created it to function. It's nothing to be ashamed of. The key is intentionality—planning ahead, setting boundaries, and understanding how to steward your desires well.

When individuals would come to me and confess, "Hey, I had sex. I'm not married, and I know that doesn't align with God's plan," I'd gently ask, "Was it good?" I wasn't trying to shock them—I was trying to disarm the shame and open a real conversation. The heart of the matter wasn't simply moral weakness—it was often a lack of intentional planning and clear boundaries to manage their desires wisely.

Desire unguarded and unplanned quickly becomes compromise, leading us places we never intended to go. Proverbs 4:27 wisely advises, "Don't get sidetracked; keep your feet from following evil" (NLT).

Let's keep it real. Emotional and physical boundaries matter, but if you're not guarding your mind, you're leaving the front door wide open. Your mind is where everything starts—your emotions, your actions, and your sense of self. If your mental boundaries aren't solid, harmful influences slip in, making your healing journey twice as hard.

DON'T DILUTE, POLLUTE, OR CONVOLUTE YOUR HEALING

Keeping your mind safe means not compromising the work you've done to find peace and get your mind right. Look at everything you've already worked on! If you're taking notes (because good nerds take notes), you've confronted trauma, healed childhood wounds, finally gotten the therapy you need, and laid the groundwork for boundaries in your relationships—that's a lot of work! Now you want to make sure you're creating a purity of thought that allows you to continue doing the work and not backtrack away from any of it. That means not diluting it, polluting it, or convoluting it.

DILUTION

Letting negativity reduce your progress is like pouring water on a fire you're trying to keep burning. Negative thoughts dilute your belief in yourself and your right to heal. So shut down negative conversations. If someone consistently brings drama, shame, or negativity into your life, politely decline their invitation to that chaos. Negative talk slowly eats away at your confidence and can pull you right back down.

Don't forget to also check your own negative thinking. Those sneaky thoughts telling you you're not enough? You gotta recognize them and shut them down quickly. Dwelling on lies traps you in unnecessary despair.

But if doubt does start to creep in, remind yourself of the following truths loud and clear:

You aren't your mistakes.
You have every right to grow.
God is working in you daily.
Your journey matters.
Progress, not perfection, is the goal.

Repeating these truths builds stronger pathways in your brain, literally rewiring it to handle life with hope and resilience. It's not just positive thinking—it's training your mind for victory.

POLLUTION

Protect your mind like it's your most valuable property—because it is. Just as you wouldn't let just anybody stroll into your house, don't let just anything into your mental space. Certain shows, conversations, or social media can mess with your peace, causing unnecessary confusion and temptation. If any shows or songs throw you back into old pain, skip them. For me, as much as folks hyped up *Game of Thrones*, I knew medieval nudity wasn't helping my mental wellness plan. No judgment—just clarity. Know what pollutes your peace, and keep that mess at the door. It ain't about running from reality—it's about protecting your peace.

CONVOLUTION

Stop making your healing harder than it needs to be. Sometimes we overthink so much that we freeze and don't make any moves. Healing can be slow and messy—and that's completely okay. Getting stuck in your head trying to figure everything out perfectly will paralyze your progress. Remember, slow steps are still real steps. You might not be stuck—you're just moving forward at your own pace. Embrace simplicity and give yourself some grace.

YOU'RE ALLOWED TO TAKE YOUR TIME

This journey toward a safe mind isn't a fast one. Whether it takes you months to speak about trauma, years to trust your therapist fully, or even longer to find peace after loss, you're right on time. Healing isn't a straight line; it's your unique journey. Comparing your healing to anyone else's steals your peace and joy. God's got your timeline, and trust me, He ain't rushing you. Be patient and kind with yourself, and allow your healing to unfold naturally and gently.

And remember that peace doesn't come from perfection; it comes from perspective. Guarding your mind doesn't mean hiding from life—it means stepping into it fully, from a place of wholeness and strength, not just survival.

If you slip along the way?

Take a deep breath.
Gently shift your thoughts.
Give it another shot.
Lean on your support system.
Remind yourself of your worth.

This isn't about quick fixes—it's about steadily building a safe space in your mind where healing, growth, and rest can happen. Not everyone or everything deserves a key to your peace. Protect your mind fiercely, because a safe mind means a stable, meaningful life.

REFLECTION QUESTIONS

1. Are unsafe thoughts creeping in?
2. What mental boundaries do I really need?
3. Am I diluting, polluting, or convoluting my journey?
4. What does a safe mental space look like for me?
5. What practical step can I take today to start protecting my mental peace?

STAGE 2

REMEMBRANCE

At this stage, the focus is to overcome the fear of traumatic memories so they can be integrated, allowing appreciation for the person you have become as a result of the trauma. In order to metabolize (not just verbalize) memories, you may make use of EMDR or other mind-body therapies. Pacing ensures that you don't become "stuck" in avoidance or overwhelmed by memories and flashbacks. Since "remembering is not recovering," the goal is to come to terms with the traumatic past.

—*Janina Fisher*[1]

15

NO LONGER A VICTIM

Once I find safety—in my body, my space, and my mind—I can start confronting the memories that once held me hostage.

That's what stage 2 of trauma recovery is all about: facing the past without becoming paralyzed by it.

Janina Fisher referenced this familiar quote: "Remembering is not recovering."

Just talking about trauma doesn't equal healing. Recalling pain isn't resolving it. Naming your history matters, but actually working through it? That's where real freedom kicks in.

Think of your brain like an old-school desktop computer. Trauma is stored in folders you can click open. But without the right tools or guidance, opening those folders can crash your entire system. Ever had a computer freeze because you clicked too many tabs open at once? Same vibe.

Remembering is a necessary step—but it isn't the finish line. If all you do is keep replaying old scenes without resolution, you get stuck in an endless loop. That's emotional self-sabotage. That's staying trapped. True recovery means discovering new, healthier ways to engage with your old stories. To actually move forward into freedom and not just talk about something from your past like it's still your present. To walk in that direction, you need to lean in to therapy.

TALK. GROUP. EMDR.

There are tons of therapy types out there, and while I'm no clinician, I can definitely break down for you what's worked best for me: one-on-one talk therapy, group therapy, and EMDR (eye movement desensitization and reprocessing).

Let's unpack these.

TALK THERAPY

Picture yourself dumping puzzle pieces onto a table. Some you instantly recognize; others you've never seen clearly before. Your therapist is the one helping you identify, organize, and connect these pieces into a bigger picture.

This isn't just emotional venting. It's deeper. It's integration. It's making sense of why things happened and how they've shaped you.

I vividly remember my very first therapy session—I didn't really know what to expect. All I knew was that I left that session with a clearer understanding of myself, my personality quirks, and even the reasons behind some of my behaviors. Just sharing my story with someone trained to help me unpack it began to change my perspective. It wasn't about getting everything fixed in one session; it was about beginning to understand myself in ways I never had before. The same thing can happen for you.

Talk therapy helps you rewrite narratives, transforming confusion into clarity and chaos into understanding. It can reveal patterns and unlock insights that help you move forward in life.

GROUP THERAPY

Group therapy was where things got incredibly real for me. Imagine seeing your life as if it were playing out on a movie set. One-on-one therapy gives you the first-person camera view, but group therapy? That's like having every camera imaginable trained on you. You've got your first-person camera, the overhead jib camera capturing everything from above, the drone footage giving you panoramic views, the steady cam weaving through intimate moments, and even cameras that zoom in to catch every subtle reaction and emotion.

When someone else shares their story, it doesn't just sit there. It resonates deeply, echoing parts of your own story—even things you've overlooked or buried. It's not even always about going through the exact same thing; sometimes it's just hearing another perspective, seeing your experience mirrored from another angle, and suddenly gaining a brand-new insight. That's group therapy: surround-sound, high-definition healing.

Here's why group therapy hits so differently:

- It reduces isolation—you realize you're not alone.
- It creates accountability—you have people who understand your struggle.
- It provides fresh perspective—your story feels validated, respected, and clearer.
- It encourages raw honesty and vulnerability, yet feels completely safe because everyone's in the same boat.

In my process group, we hold space for each other without judgment or unsolicited advice. It's presence, pure and simple. Think about holding back a friend's hair while they're sick—that's the level of care and attentiveness. It's intense, emotional, and sacred. People heal in groups because we were never meant to navigate life alone. When God said, "It is not good for the man to be alone" (Gen. 2:18

NLT), it wasn't just about marriage—it was about community. We thrive and heal through relationships. Group therapy taps into that divine design, and, honestly, it became my lifeline.

EMDR

EMDR might sound like something crazy, but trust me, it's legit clinical therapy and genuinely transformative. Let's clear the air, though, because EMDR has gotten a bit of a shaky reputation—not because there's something fundamentally wrong with it, but mostly due to misunderstandings or bad experiences with specific practitioners. But think about it: You can have a bad experience at a doctor's office, the dentist, or even your favorite barber. That doesn't mean the entire industry is flawed—just that one experience or person.

EMDR stands for "eye movement desensitization and reprocessing." Here's the straightforward breakdown of how it works: A trained therapist guides you through traumatic memories while simultaneously having you perform specific eye movements, tap gently, or listen to rhythmic sounds. This is known as "bilateral stimulation," and it helps your brain reprocess those traumatic experiences. Think of it like sorting through a messy file cabinet—EMDR helps organize your memories so they're stored without the intense emotional charge. This allows you to recall the memories without your nervous system launching into fight, flight, or freeze mode.

Now, let's be crystal-clear: You won't come out hypnotized or under any spell. EMDR isn't magic; it's neuroscience at work. It's safe, it's grounded in scientific research, and, honestly, it can even feel spiritual because it aligns your mind, body, and emotions in ways few other therapies can.

For me personally, EMDR was a game changer. It helped me zero in on core traumatic events, neutralizing their impact. The result? I could finally share my story without reexperiencing the intense emotions and physical sensations that used to accompany it. EMDR allowed me to remember without reliving, giving me back the narrative control over my own life.

The same can happen for you. EMDR isn't something to fear—it's something to embrace. Done right, EMDR can significantly reduce anxiety, eliminate chronic triggers, and restore your emotional balance, helping you finally reclaim your peace.

YES, YOU CAN

Let's get something straight. Therapy isn't always encouraged in certain families or cultures. Maybe you grew up hearing, "We don't talk about that," "Keep this within the family," or "We don't air our family business." Perhaps you've heard whispers like, "You'll ruin everything if you tell."

Why do people say these things? Often it's because they're afraid of judgment or losing respect in their community. They fear shame and stigma, worrying about how their family will be perceived. Some believe that discussing personal pain or trauma makes the family look weak or flawed. In other cases, people genuinely think they're protecting one another by keeping silent—believing that facing the truth openly might fracture relationships or cause irreparable harm. These fears have built deep-rooted systems of silence within families, keeping pain hidden and healing delayed.

I'm here to dismantle that mindset, because it's a flat-out lie.

Therapy is not a sign of weakness—it's a clear sign of strength. Every great boxer has a coach, not because they're weak but because they want to win. Every champion athlete has a trainer because they know reaching greatness requires expert support. Every person serious about their health consults a nutritionist because wise decisions demand guidance. As with these other professionals, having a therapist means you're strong enough to seek clarity, guidance, and growth for your emotional and mental well-being. It shows you are courageous enough to confront challenges head-on, resilient enough to unpack tough truths, and committed to your own well-being enough to ask for help. Seeking therapy is an act of bravery, a decisive step toward reclaiming control of your life and emotions.

Here's the truth: You can heal. You can grow. You absolutely can do this work. You are resilient enough to face your challenges. You deserve to reclaim your joy and peace.

No matter how long you've carried the pain, how deeply you've buried your feelings, or who told you otherwise—you can find healing. You deserve support. You deserve freedom. The choice is yours. Take the step, because you're worth it.

GENERATIONAL SHIFT STARTS WITH YOU

Exodus 12:14 instructs God's people to commemorate their day of deliverance: "This is a day to remember. . . . From generation to generation, you must celebrate it as a special festival to the LORD" (NLT).

God didn't just free the Israelites from slavery in Egypt; He wanted them to mark that freedom so clearly that it became a generational inheritance. He wanted their descendants to inherit stories of deliverance, not captivity.

Imagine this:

What broke your grandfather doesn't have to break you.
What wounded your father doesn't have to wound your children.
What silenced your lineage can now sing freedom over future generations.
What trapped your mother doesn't have to confine your daughters.

What bound your ancestors doesn't have to chain your descendants.

Your healing isn't just personal—it's powerful enough to shift generations. By actively engaging in your recovery, you're writing a new story for your family. One that doesn't echo cycles of pain but celebrates cycles of triumph. You are the bridge from past struggles to future strengths.

This isn't about perfection—it's about legacy. Often when we talk about legacy, we think about leaving money or property. But what if the greatest inheritance you could pass on wasn't financial but emotional and spiritual? Imagine if your legacy was peace. Think about it: Jesus said in John 14:27, "Peace I leave with you, My peace I give to you; not as the world gives do I give to you. Let not your heart be troubled, neither let it be afraid." In other words, "I am leaving you with a gift—peace of mind and heart." If this was Jesus's most precious gift, shouldn't it be ours as well?

Your courage to heal today becomes the legacy your children carry tomorrow. Your resilience sets a foundation for those who come after you, teaching them how to rise and recover. Your vulnerability dismantles generational secrets, empowering transparency and open dialogue for the generations that follow.

Your healing journey holds the key to unlocking profound generational shifts. Start now, because your freedom matters—not just for you but for everyone coming after you. Why wait? Why put this burden on your children or grandchildren? Why blame your parents when you hold the power to break these cycles? Why not you? Why not now?

This is your moment. Your decision to heal is prophetic, declaring to future generations that pain does not have the final say. Your healing can become their normal. Make your mark, start the shift, and watch how your courage transforms not just your life but countless lives yet to come.

NO LONGER A VICTIM

Recovery doesn't erase the past—it teaches you to carry the story without collapsing. It empowers you to discuss your trauma without dissociating or disconnecting, acknowledge your pain without drowning in despair, and face your shame without feeling stuck there.

When you drop the victim mentality, amazing things start to happen:

Your brain stops replaying the trauma loop endlessly.
Your confidence and self-esteem gradually rebuild.
You see opportunities for growth instead of just setbacks.
Relationships become healthier because you stop projecting unresolved issues onto others.
You take back control of your emotional well-being.
You experience a newfound freedom to define yourself beyond your trauma.
Your resilience strengthens, enabling you to face challenges head-on.
Your emotional responses become more regulated and grounded.

You're not defined by what happened—you define yourself by how you respond, heal, and move forward. Life is different now because you're no longer allowing your past to pollute your present or sabotage your future. You find yourself more present in daily interactions, fully engaging in life rather than constantly bracing for impact. Your energy shifts from living in survival mode to thriving, giving you space to explore passions, dreams, and possibilities you once thought impossible. Stress becomes manageable and peace becomes accessible, even in previously triggering environments. You're able to build deeper, more authentic connections because trust and vulnerability replace fear and defensiveness. Your newfound clarity and emotional intelligence create a ripple effect, positively influencing those around you. This transformation doesn't just benefit you—it becomes a beacon of hope and healing for others on their journeys.

So start your healing journey right now. Don't wait another day. Look up therapists in your area using resources like *Psychology Today* or counseling centers nearby, or even check out local churches—some offer free Christian counseling for members. Ask your friends or trusted individuals for recommendations; you might be surprised how many people around you have already taken the step toward improving their mental health.

If logistics or finances seem like obstacles, we've got you covered. Visit the Balm Counseling Center, an accessible online platform we've created to remove barriers to mental health support. Additionally, explore Mentor U, our mentorship platform, all available at UpsetTheWorld.com.

If you're completely new to therapy or mental health support, consider watching or listening to *The Basement* podcast, where we've built safe spaces to have authentic, meaningful conversations one-on-one. You can also tune in to our weekly live three-hour podcast, *The Basement Live*, where two of those hours are dedicated exclusively to real-time calls from around the world, as I help people process life's challenges in community. We've also created a vibrant Discord community of seven thousand members committed to making peace their inheritance and vulnerability their birthright.

Remember, whether you work with us or choose someone else, the most important step is simply to start. Your journey matters deeply. Your peace matters profoundly. Healing is not only possible—it's ready and waiting for you today. Take the first step and reclaim the joy and clarity you deserve.

REFLECTION QUESTIONS

1. Am I still holding on to a victim identity?
2. Have I started therapy—or is something holding me back?
3. Which memories am I ready to face and reprocess?
4. Practically, what does breaking generational cycles look like for me?
5. What actionable step can I take right now toward my recovery journey?

16

LIFE BE LIFEIN'

Healing isn't about forgetting. It's about learning to speak your story without drowning in pain each time.

This is the heartbeat of stage 2 in recovery: remembering without reliving. Reflecting without unraveling. And yeah—I know I mentioned this before. I might even sound like a broken record. But listen: This stage is critical. It's the pivot point between surviving and thriving, and I want you to get this deep into your bones.

Let's keep it 100: Starting therapy doesn't stop life from throwing curveballs. Your challenges don't pause because you're healing. Life doesn't check your calendar or wait for your permission. It keeps rolling in waves—unexpected bills, relationship tensions, job losses, health scares. But therapy equips you to navigate those waves differently. Instead of getting knocked over by them, you learn to surf—to stay balanced even when the waters get rough.

Recently, I asked my homie how he was. He just shrugged, laughed a little, and said, "Man, life be lifein'."

That hit me right in the chest. Because life does exactly that—it just keeps happening. There are valleys and storms. Breakups and layoffs. Betrayals and disappointments. Diagnoses and deaths.

Maybe you were like me and grew up hearing messages that painted life as a perpetual spiritual obstacle course, designed by God to challenge and test us at every turn, measuring our devotion by how well we navigated pain. But as I've matured, I've realized this perspective is deeply flawed.

Does suffering test our devotion? Yes, absolutely. But who exactly is handing out these tests? Is it truly God intentionally setting traps and hurdles just to see whether we measure up, or is it simply life—filled with unpredictability, complexity, and, yes, pain—testing us naturally?

I firmly believe that God did not set up life as some insurmountable obstacle course so He could watch from above to see whether we'll fail or succeed. Instead, He promises His constant presence in the midst of life's inherent difficulties. Life itself brings enough tests and trials without attributing our suffering to God's hand. He doesn't inflict tragedy to refine our character. Rather, He commits to walking alongside us, guiding us, comforting us, and strengthening us through every challenge we face.

Life doesn't pause till you feel strong enough to handle those trials. It won't wait till you've memorized more verses. But healing helps us learn to walk with God and handle the hits without falling apart.

Let's unpack this clearly, because many have been sold the lie that choosing to follow Yeshua (Jesus) somehow exempts us from life's struggles. I've seen folks shocked, almost offended, when hardships hit after they've surrendered their lives to God, like "Hold up! Didn't I sign up for blessings only?" But the truth is that God never promised exemption from life's troubles—He promised companionship in them.

Life won't politely pause for your prayers to catch up. It won't hold back storms until you feel spiritually equipped. Memorizing Scripture is powerful, but it's not a shield from pain—it's a lifeline through it. Healing isn't about living untouched; it's about having the tools and support to stay whole when life inevitably touches you. Real faith doesn't deny difficulty—it acknowledges the mess and walks right through it with God at your side.

PAUL DIDN'T MINIMIZE HIS TRAUMA

Paul gave one of the most trauma-informed testimonies you'll ever read, in 2 Corinthians 11:25: "Three times I was beaten with rods; once I was stoned; three times I was shipwrecked; a night and a day I have been in the deep." Flogged. Imprisoned. Shipwrecked. Betrayed. Starved. Beaten. Cold. Hunted. Rejected.

Yet Paul didn't spiral or get hijacked by his memories. He was honest, vulnerable, real—yet grounded. He didn't make trauma the center. He made God the anchor.

Paul's testimony shows us the difference between scars and wounds. Scars speak of healing; wounds speak of hurt. Paul spoke from scars, not open wounds.

Let's break down this crucial difference: An open wound is still fresh. It hasn't healed yet, which means it's sensitive, easily irritated, and at risk of further damage. Touching an open wound hurts deeply, often reopening the trauma and risking infection. Similarly, speaking from an open emotional wound means reliving pain, possibly causing yourself and others harm or confusion.

A scar, on the other hand, is evidence of healing. It's tougher skin that forms after the wound has closed. Scars show where you've been, but they don't hurt when touched. They can even become powerful testimonies—visible proof that what hurt you didn't destroy you. Scars don't bleed; they speak. They narrate a story of survival, resilience, and healing.

Paul was showing us his scars—not to showcase suffering but to highlight the depth of God's faithfulness. His scars pointed to healing, growth, and victory, never confusion or ongoing pain.

INFLUENCE VS. INFECTION

Too many leaders today build platforms from pain they haven't healed. That's not influence—it's infection.

Influence flows from healed places. It means remembering without unraveling, speaking truth without bleeding over others.

Shared wounds aren't true community. Commiseration isn't transformation. Your pain is real, but it can't become your identity. Too many people today dive shallowly into mental health, splashing around without ever going deep enough to truly heal. Instead, they stay stuck celebrating their brokenness, rehashing pain, and calling it authenticity. But authenticity isn't merely owning your wounds—it's pursuing genuine healing until those wounds become scars that inspire rather than infect.

Paul wore his scars not as badges of brokenness but as proof that God's faithfulness carried him through. Let's clarify this, because the distinction between influence and infection matters. Influence uplifts and strengthens. It comes from a place of restoration, bringing clarity and genuine encouragement. When you share from your healed scars, you impart hope and resilience to others. Your experiences become sources of wisdom and empowerment. Here's what healthy, uplifting influence looks like in practical leadership:

Leaders transparently share lessons learned without triggering their teams.

- They cultivate environments where vulnerability leads to actionable growth and trust.
- They encourage resilience and healthy coping strategies in the face of setbacks.
- They model accountability, humility, and continuous personal growth.
- They prioritize clear, calm communication that stabilizes rather than stirs up anxiety.

Infection, however, spreads unresolved trauma. It creates confusion, breeds stagnation, and can unintentionally perpetuate cycles of hurt. Leaders speaking from wounds that haven't healed risk replicating their traumas, fostering communities stuck in shared pain rather than moving them toward true healing. Here's what that kind of unhealthy, infectious leadership looks like practically:

- Leaders frequently vent unresolved personal issues, creating anxious team dynamics.
- They encourage emotional reactions without offering clear solutions or direction.
- They allow personal trauma to bias decision-making, harming organizational clarity.
- They foster a culture where shared struggles become a perpetual echo chamber of complaints rather than growth.
- They lead from a place of emotional volatility, creating instability and inconsistency in team environments.

Authentic community fosters growth, healing, and forward movement—not perpetual commiseration. Real influence transforms pain into purposeful testimony, turning our scars into powerful narratives of recovery and divine faithfulness.

GOD DOESN'T JUST WATCH US—GOD IS WITH US

I once believed trauma was God's way of testing me—each tragedy an exam in faith. Growing up, I heard so much preaching that every painful life circumstance was God putting us through trials to gain glory from our suffering. But Scripture reveals something completely different:

- "The LORD is close to the brokenhearted; he rescues those whose spirits are crushed" (Ps. 34:18 NLT).
- "Give all your worries and cares to God, for he cares about you" (1 Peter 5:7 NLT).
- "Come to me, all of you who are weary and carry heavy burdens, and I will give you rest" (Matt. 11:28 NLT).

During a powerful therapy session, I revisited the very first time I was sexually abused by the neighbor who lived across the street. My therapist gently but firmly asked, "Where do you see Jesus in this moment?"

Initially, in my mind, Jesus appeared close by, just watching, shaking His head sadly as He said, "I didn't want this to happen to you, but I'll use it for My glory." But my therapist felt something was off and said, "Let's pray again. God, Creator of the universe, show Tim clearly where You truly were when he was being abused."

This time, the image shifted dramatically. The figure initially thought to be Jesus was revealed to be an angel of darkness—a deceptive presence making me think Jesus was distant and passively observing my pain.

In the next moment, Jesus wasn't standing on the sidelines. Instead, He was me. He was right there, being abused with me. Bearing every moment of my trauma alongside me. It became clear: When Jesus bore the sins of the world, He didn't just bear our wrongdoing—He bore every wrong done to us. Every assault. Every betrayal. Every trauma.

That revelation shattered my theology. It broke apart the old, harmful ideas that painted God as distant or as a divine orchestrator of pain. My theology shifted dramatically and permanently.

Jesus didn't just die for my sins; He absorbed every abuse, carried every trauma inflicted upon me—upon us. He didn't simply witness our pain from afar; He entered it. He experienced it. He carries it with us. He shares every step intimately.

God is not watching our suffering passively—He's actively walking through it with us.

I no longer try to spiritualize every hardship. I've lived too long and seen too much to believe everything has a deep spiritual explanation. I've watched faithful friends die too young, sat with grieving families, seen righteous people face injustice, watched good people file for bankruptcy, witnessed others suffer severe car accidents, seen folks swindled out of their life savings, observed people caught up in internet scams, dealt with unexpected job losses, and seen loving families torn apart by misunderstandings.

Sometimes the only answer is simply "Life be lifein'." But there's a deeper truth that sustains us: God is always right there, steady and close.

The clear promise of Psalm 23 comforts us: "Yea, though I walk through the valley of the shadow of death, I will fear no evil: for thou art with me" (v. 4 KJV). Jesus affirmed this promise, saying, "Lo, I am with you always, even unto the end of the world" (Matt. 28:20 KJV).

He promised His presence and peace above all else. He didn't promise exemption from hardship; He promised companionship through it.

God isn't orchestrating your pain to teach you something. He's faithfully walking beside you through every valley, every storm. And knowing that makes it just a little bit easier to let that pain become a scar and not an open wound.

RETELLING WITHOUT RELIVING

I once thought healing meant never crying again when telling my story.

I was wrong.

Healing means I can cry and still breathe deeply. I can mourn and remain anchored. It means the past doesn't trap me—I can visit without drowning.

This truth is so important that I'm intentionally repeating it again. Retelling your story without reliving it is foundational to genuine healing. It's not about avoiding emotions; it's about managing them effectively. Two things can be true simultaneously: You can feel pain deeply, yet not be overwhelmed or consumed by it.

This is precisely what therapy—especially EMDR—gifted me: the powerful ability to remember without reexperiencing trauma as if it's happening all over again.

Being a trauma-informed person of faith means recognizing that Scripture itself is profoundly trauma informed. From Genesis 3 onward, the Bible openly acknowledges pain, trauma, and brokenness. It doesn't deny or minimize human suffering. Instead, it provides stories, psalms, and wisdom that guide us through healing journeys with compassion and clarity.

Trauma-informed faith anchors me in the present—clear-eyed, steady-hearted, emotionally mature, and spiritually rooted. It equips me to navigate life's storms without losing sight of God's enduring presence and peace.

TESTIMONY, NOT TRAUMA DUMP

My desire is for my story to become a clear testimony, not a trauma loop. Like Paul, I want my scars to speak of God's goodness—not of confusion or chaos. I want to recall without re-wounding. That's why I intentionally do the work—real, dedicated work. I partner closely with therapists who help me navigate the depths of my story safely. I invite Jesus into each memory, every scene of pain to illuminate and transform my perspective. I actively practice nervous-system regulation to ensure I stay grounded and safe while sharing my story. And I reject the harmful idea that ongoing pain somehow equates to greater faithfulness.

In this season my calling is to normalize vulnerability—to live authentically as someone fully seen, fully heard, fully known, and fully loved, even if not fully agreed with. My testimony is not about pouring raw, unresolved trauma onto others. It's not about bleeding out emotionally in public spaces. Instead, I show healed scars while others may still bear open wounds, demonstrating practically and lovingly that healing is possible. I share my story not to retraumatize or overwhelm but to inspire hope, healing, and transformation. My scars become powerful testimonies, beautiful reminders of the Lord's unwavering faithfulness, rather than loops of ongoing pain and despair. And you can have the same thing.

What happened to you doesn't define you. Your response to those events is what shapes your identity.

You're not defined by your past trauma. You're not permanently labeled by what someone else did to you. You have the power and permission to rewrite your narrative into something beautiful, hopeful, and meaningful. You aren't merely surviving; you're on a powerful journey toward thriving. This new identity can bring profound freedom and joy.

Imagine a life where your experiences serve as stepping stones rather than stumbling blocks. Visualize relationships built on mutual respect and trust, careers that flourish because you're fully present, and personal fulfillment rooted in healed self-awareness. You have every reason to be excited about your new identity. This identity isn't trapped by history but freed by healing. This identity allows you to live boldly, love deeply, and hope fearlessly. This identity is yours to discover, embrace, and celebrate fully.

FREEDOM IS GENERATIONAL

Exodus 12:14 says clearly, "This is a day to remember. . . . Generation to generation, you must celebrate it" (NLT).

We touched on this powerful idea in chapter 15, but it's so crucial we need to revisit it from another angle. Freedom isn't just an individual moment—it's generational. We have the extraordinary privilege to either inherit freedom or become the pioneers who establish it for future generations. The freedom we cultivate today can create generational blessings that ripple out to touch thousands of future descendants.

Consider what generational freedom looks like practically: It can mean breaking cycles of addiction so your children and grandchildren grow up in sober, peaceful homes. It can mean overcoming financial trauma to establish generational wealth, financial literacy, and stability. It could look like ending cycles of emotional or physical abuse, ensuring your descendants live in safe, loving environments. Perhaps it's choosing therapy and emotional health today so future generations grow up with healthier communication skills and emotional resilience.

Your choice to heal doesn't only change your story—it changes the story for everyone who follows. It reshapes family dynamics, establishes healthier traditions, and creates a foundation of strength, resilience, and emotional wellness.

Maybe you're the one rewriting your family's story. The cycle breaker. The therapy-goer. The boundary-setter. The healed one.

At family reunions, you might stand out. You might find yourself becoming the "peace sheep"—not the black sheep. Your aunties might side-eye your peace. Your cousins might clown your healthy boundaries. It might feel awkward, even uncomfortable, as you shift the rhythm of your family gatherings.

But here's the beauty: You were never meant to blend seamlessly into dysfunction. You're meant to transform it, challenge it, and model a healthier way. Being the free strand might mean you're the odd one out—but that's precisely how it should be. If your peace and wellness stand in stark contrast to generational dysfunction, you're on the right path.

Smile anyway. Celebrate your freedom. You're the free strand, the example of what's possible, and that's something worth standing proudly in.

REFLECTION QUESTIONS

1. Am I retelling or reliving my story?
2. What parts of my past still hijack my present?
3. What does it look like to metabolize a memory?
4. Where have I clearly seen Jesus with me in my pain?
5. What narrative needs rewriting today?

17

THE RELAPSE

Even while we're walking this freeing journey to healing, I want to acknowledge that there will be times when we experience a setback. Like I've said before, healing isn't linear. Recovery doesn't always move in a straight line. And relapse isn't failure—it's feedback.

Sometimes our bodies remember the familiar flavor of past coping mechanisms, and before we know it, we find ourselves craving Egypt again—not because Egypt was beneficial, but simply because it felt familiar. Familiarity often feels safer, even if it's harmful.

This is a sobering reality as we journey toward stage 3 in trauma recovery. Relapse, setbacks, and stumbles are not evidence that we've failed or aren't healing correctly—they are natural aspects of growth and recovery. As with a toddler learning to walk, falling isn't failing—it's learning. Each fall informs the next step, strengthens muscles, and builds balance. Similarly, in trauma recovery, each relapse provides valuable feedback, highlighting areas where deeper healing is needed. It invites us to offer ourselves compassion, adjust our approach, and keep moving forward, step by steady step.

GOD BROUGHT THEM OUT—BUT HE DIDN'T RUSH THEM IN

When God delivered Israel from Egypt, He didn't lead them straight into the promised land. Instead, He brought them into the wilderness—not as punishment, but as preparation.

In Messianic Jewish thought, the wilderness holds deep spiritual and symbolic significance. The Hebrew word for "wilderness," "*midbar*," shares its root with "*davar*," meaning "word" or "speak." Thus, the wilderness represents a place of divine communication and clarity, free from distractions and familiar comforts.

The wilderness was Israel's rehab center, their detox unit, their nervous-system reset. It was essential that Israel not simply transition from slavery directly into a promised paradise, because abrupt changes without preparation can cause their own type of trauma. Instantaneous transitions rarely sustain healing or growth.

Why the wilderness?

Because Israel had spent four hundred years immersed in trauma.

They understood oppression intimately, but freedom was entirely foreign.

They were conditioned by a harsh, oppressive master; the concept of a loving, nurturing Father was completely unknown.

Fear had become their default reaction, deeply ingrained into their nervous systems; trust was something new and unfamiliar.

God intentionally created this expansive, quiet, isolated space to help them unlearn slavery and relearn freedom. It was not only physical freedom they needed to grasp but also mental, emotional, and spiritual liberation. They needed time and space to heal from the accumulated stress and trauma, time to retrain their instincts and learn to receive provision from a place of trust rather than fear.

The wilderness was not a place of abandonment but rather an intentional environment of intimate alignment. Here, separated from the chains and trauma triggers of Egypt, the Israelites had the opportunity to listen to and clearly hear from God. In this quiet and desolate space, distractions were removed, allowing them to receive divine instruction, the Torah, and God's covenantal promises directly from Him. The wilderness became their sacred classroom, where God carefully and patiently taught them how to relate to Him, trust Him, and depend upon Him.

This concept is similar to modern-day spiritual retreats. Today, people willingly choose to go on retreats where they intentionally strip themselves of comforts, leaving behind technology, familiar routines, and daily distractions. These retreats often happen in remote, quiet places without cell service, amenities, or modern conveniences. Participants willingly isolate themselves to clearly hear and reconnect with God, seeking deeper alignment and spiritual clarity.

The wilderness was a reset button for the Israelites' identities, redefining who they were—no longer slaves but children of God, chosen and dearly loved. It was in this barren land that they began to shed old identities formed by pain and oppression, gradually stepping into the freedom and wholeness God intended. Imagine this: an entire nation summoned by God Himself to participate in the ultimate spiritual retreat—an opportunity to step away, reset, and realign with their divine purpose.

There, He gave them manna. Not steak. Not leeks. Not onions. Just enough daily nourishment to reset their tastes, recalibrate their appetites, realign their trust, and ultimately reestablish their entire way of being. Manna symbolized the steady, predictable provision from a caring Father. It wasn't extravagant or flashy; it was consistent and faithful—exactly what their traumatized hearts and minds needed most to stabilize, heal, and flourish.

Manna often gets a bad rap for being bland. But that blandness was intentional. It served as sacred transitional food, carefully chosen by God to neutralize the lingering effects of Egypt's trauma and prepare their palates for the rich abundance of milk and honey awaiting them in the promised land.

Consider how deeply the tastes and flavors of Egypt were tied to their bondage. The garlic, leeks, onions, and savory meats weren't just foods—they were daily reminders of the harsh conditions of their captivity. Even their appetites were linked to their trauma, reinforcing a deeply ingrained cycle of oppression and survival.

In terms of trauma recovery, manna played a crucial and deliberate role. It was regulatory—steady, predictable, stabilizing nourishment. It wasn't flashy or intensely flavorful, because the Israelites' nervous systems didn't need more sensory stimulation. They didn't need seasoning; they needed sustenance. They needed consistency and dependability, something predictable that would soothe their overstimulated minds and stabilize their anxious hearts.

That's precisely why relapse can feel so disorienting. The nourishing simplicity of God's provision often pales in comparison to the intense, dopamine-triggering experiences of our past traumas. It's natural to crave the excitement and intensity of past coping mechanisms, even if they came with chains attached. Our nervous systems remember the temporary highs, the brief moments of escape from pain, and we mistakenly equate that intensity with safety or comfort.

But God, in His wisdom, knows that real healing isn't found in returning to what enslaved us. Freedom and healing are cultivated in the quiet, gentle, steady nourishment that resets and stabilizes us. Like manna, God's provision in our recovery might initially seem dull compared to the excitement of our pasts, but its purpose is profound—anchoring us in genuine peace, stability, and long-term growth.

SELECTIVE MEMORY IS A SYMPTOM OF RELAPSE

In Numbers 11:5–6, the Israelites complained, "We remember the fish we used to eat for free in Egypt. . . . But now our appetites are gone. All we ever see is this manna!" (NLT).

"For free"? They were enslaved.

Did they forget the brutal reality of their bondage?

Did they not remember how their backs were whipped raw and torn open under the scorching Egyptian sun? Had they forgotten the cries and wails of their mothers, sisters, and daughters, who faced unspeakable abuse? Did they erase the humiliating pain of being forced to make bricks without straw, the endless hours of hard labor that left their bodies broken and weary? How quickly did they overlook the ruthless exploitation, the relentless oppression, the crushing burden placed on their shoulders every single day.

Trauma has a powerful, deceptive way of rewriting history, glamorizing the very things that nearly destroyed us:

We remember the thrill, but not the devastating crash.
We recall the excitement, but conveniently forget the manipulation.
We savor the taste, yet ignore the chains that accompanied it.
We cherish fleeting pleasure, ignoring lasting pain.
We romanticize toxic relationships, forgetting emotional abuse.
We idolize momentary highs but erase memories of deep lows.
We embrace familiar chaos, overlooking the anxiety it brought.
We reminisce about comfort foods, ignoring the health issues they caused.
We nostalgically remember our former lifestyles, dismissing their destructive outcomes.

We relive memories of intense connection, neglecting the resulting isolation.
We dwell on quick fixes, forgetting their long-term consequences.

Selective memory blinds us to reality. Healing requires facing truth head-on, remembering the full story—not just the appealing highlights but also the harsh, sobering facts.

WHO'S WHISPERING AT YOUR TABLE?

The Bible notes it wasn't just Israelites craving Egypt; it was the "foreign rabble" traveling with them (Num. 11:4 NLT). In Exodus 12:38, this "mixed multitude" refers to individuals who weren't Israelites by birth but left Egypt alongside Israel, perhaps drawn by the miracles they witnessed or simply seeking freedom from their own oppression. But they lacked the same covenantal relationship with God, cultural history, and spiritual foundation as Israel. Their presence became problematic because their cravings and complaints deeply influenced and destabilized the community.

This matters profoundly in your healing journey. Not everyone traveling alongside you shares your goals or understands the depth of your commitment to recovery. Some people may initially seem supportive, but beneath the surface their motivations, maturity levels, or unresolved issues can inadvertently sabotage your progress. They might unintentionally minimize your experiences, offer misguided advice, or project their own struggles onto your path. These individuals may genuinely believe they're helping, yet their lack of true alignment or emotional maturity can create confusion and setbacks, potentially leading you toward old patterns instead of reinforcing new, healthy habits. Recognizing and setting boundaries around these relationships isn't about rejecting anyone—it's about protecting the sacred work of your healing and growth.

When breaking free from addiction, trauma, or destructive patterns, the wrong voices can trivialize relapse, making it seem minor or harmless:

> "One drink won't hurt."
> "It's just this one time."
> "Relax, you're too uptight."
> "You've been doing so well, you deserve a little break."
> "Nobody's perfect. Don't be so hard on yourself."
> "Come on, don't isolate yourself."
> "This isn't even that serious; everyone slips sometimes."
> "Life is too short not to enjoy yourself occasionally."
> "You're overthinking this—just have some fun."
> "Everyone else is doing it—one time won't set you back."

These voices, however, aren't there when the consequences unfold—the spiral into guilt, the resurgence of shame, or the painful setbacks in your progress. Your circle influences your recovery because they shape your environment, your mindset, and your emotional safety.

The people you surround yourself with should be carefully chosen—not because you're judgmental or fearful but because you are committed to your healing. Healthy circles encourage accountability, offer empathy, celebrate progress, and consistently reinforce healthy boundaries and behaviors. Your circle should amplify your growth, provide safe spaces for vulnerability, and uplift your victories, no matter how small they might seem. Choose wisely, because those closest to you can either strengthen your recovery or weaken your resolve.

WHEN I FORGOT GOD'S FAITHFULNESS

Early in my recovery journey, I worked for an electric company that was just eight minutes away from my apartment by car. But since I didn't have a car, I relied on public transportation. What would've been a quick car ride was a grueling forty-minute bus journey, full of stops, starts, and detours.

One scorching summer day, I found myself standing at the bus stop hot and exhausted, grass stuck uncomfortably in my shoes from trekking across medians to reach the stop. Sweat trickled down my face as I impatiently waited. At that very moment, a sleek car rolled up and paused at the red light right in front of me. The bass from the speakers vibrated the pavement beneath my feet. Inside, a young guy, carefree and smiling, sat confidently behind the wheel. Beside him, two beautiful women laughed, their joy loud and vibrant. They were completely oblivious to the inner turmoil I felt.

Instantly, envy surged through me. It wasn't just jealousy—it was anger, frustration, resentment. My heart began to vent silently, angrily questioning God: "Why me, Lord? Why am I struggling so much just to do the right thing, to live the way You've called me to? This dude here gets to roll around with two women, bumping his music, looking blessed, and here I am barely scraping by, just trying to hold on to hope. I don't even want two girls—I'm just trying to find one!"

I was young, around twenty-one, feeling petty and completely justified in my pouting. But at that moment I began to mentally relapse. I lost sight of God's consistent provision and kindness toward me. I forgot how He had brought me safely to Texas, rescuing me from the environmental trauma of my past life in California. I disregarded the job He had provided, the stable foundation He was meticulously constructing in my life.

Relapse isn't always physical—it often starts emotionally,

mentally, and spiritually. It creeps into our thoughts subtly, distorting our perceptions and stealing away our gratitude. In that brief moment, envy had clouded my mind, leading me dangerously close to forgetting God's faithful track record in my life.

Psalm 111:1–4 profoundly states, "He causes us to remember His wonderful works. How gracious and merciful is our LORD!" (NLT).

My memory ain't short—I often say this when reflecting on the good deeds people have done for me. If that's my attitude toward human acts of kindness, how much more should it be true of my relationship with God? The reality is that memory is not accidental—it's intentional and sacred. It shapes our journeys of recovery and helps us sustain our healing.

Throughout the books of Exodus, Leviticus, Numbers, and Deuteronomy, God repeatedly instructed the children of Israel to "remember." In these foundational books alone, the concept of remembering is emphasized at least sixteen times. Why this repetition? Because God knows how easily we forget. The Israelites continually needed reminders to anchor their identity in His past faithfulness so they could secure their trust in His future promises. God's insistence on remembrance wasn't simply to preserve history; it was a deliberate strategy to maintain spiritual and emotional health, preventing the cycle of relapse into old patterns of disbelief and rebellion.

The apostle Paul emphasized this same spiritual discipline in Philippians 4:6, instructing us to "be anxious for nothing, but in everything by prayer and supplication, with thanksgiving, let your requests be made known to God." Notice the critical role of thanksgiving—it's a powerful act rooted in memory. To genuinely thank someone, you must recall precisely what they've done for you. True gratitude requires a vivid, deliberate act of remembrance.

In our personal recovery journeys, we must actively choose what we rehearse:

I was abused, but God sustained me.

I was addicted, but God delivered me.

I was suicidal, but God rescued me.

My marriage shattered, but God restored it.

These aren't passive recollections—they're intentional acts of gratitude and affirmation. Each memory, carefully recalled, becomes a spiritual anchor. Every act of remembering strengthens our trust, reinforces our identity, and positions us to face current challenges with confidence and clarity.

Choosing to remember His faithfulness doesn't erase pain but transforms it into purpose, reinforcing hope and empowering us with courage for every step forward.

DON'T REHEARSE THE WOUND—RETELL THE VICTORY

When we center our pain, we relive it. Pain becomes our defining narrative, a recurring loop that traps us emotionally and spiritually. Each recounting reinforces the trauma, deepening the grooves of hurt, keeping wounds open and bleeding. Yet when we choose instead to center ourselves around God's presence, something profound occurs. We begin healing because His presence provides perspective, comfort, and restoration. Focusing on God transforms our pain from a cycle of despair into stepping stones of growth, resilience, and spiritual maturity.

Paul powerfully exemplified this truth in Philippians 4:11–13: "Not that I was ever in need, for I have learned how to be content with whatever I have. I know how to live on almost nothing or with everything. I have learned the secret of living in every situation, whether it is with a full stomach or empty, with plenty or little. For I can do everything through Christ, who gives me strength" (NLT).

This declaration by Paul wasn't about achieving personal ambitions or conquering worldly goals; it was about cultivating an inner state of peace, resilience, and steadfastness. Paul didn't develop contentment overnight. It came through numerous trials, victories, hardships, abundance, and scarcity. He experienced extremes of comfort and distress, satisfaction and longing. Through it all, he discovered a secret: His contentment wasn't dependent on external conditions but was rooted in his relationship with Messiah Yeshua.

By relying fully on Christ's strength, Paul learned how to stay anchored and steady even when circumstances violently shifted beneath him. His contentment was not passive resignation—it was active trust, deeply anchored in the certainty of God's sustaining presence. As with Paul, our ability to claim we "can do everything" isn't about triumphing over life's challenges by our own strength but about enduring and overcoming because of the continuous, empowering presence of God within us. It's about remaining grounded and hopeful, anchored securely to a strength beyond our own.

REFRAMING THE SETBACK

Setbacks in recovery aren't just inevitable—they're essential. At first glance relapse feels like stumbling backward, but from a broader perspective it's often a hidden gateway to deeper healing.

When the Israelites struggled in the wilderness, their setbacks weren't isolated incidents of rebellion; they were critical moments revealing their true heart conditions. Similarly, our own setbacks can serve as profound mirrors, reflecting unaddressed needs and unresolved wounds. Setbacks don't reveal weakness—they uncover areas God lovingly desires to heal more fully.

Consider Peter, who denied Yeshua three times. That setback was painful, humiliating, and heartbreaking. Yet it wasn't the end of Peter's story. It became the very place where Yeshua restored him, reinforcing Peter's identity and calling him into deeper relationship and purpose (John 21:15–17). Your setbacks can likewise become sacred ground for encounter, restoration, and a strengthened identity in God.

What matters is not the relapse itself but how we respond to it. Will we let shame dictate our next steps, or will we choose vulnerability and invite God into the very place we stumbled?

Here's how we can practically reframe setbacks as opportunities:

- **PAUSE WITH PURPOSE:** When a relapse occurs, don't rush past it. Pause to acknowledge and identify what triggered it.
- **INVITE REFLECTION:** Engage intentionally with reflection or journaling, exploring the underlying needs or pains that surfaced during the relapse.
- **SEEK SUPPORT:** Reach out immediately to safe, trusted community or professional counselors who can offer insight without judgment.
- **REAFFIRM IDENTITY:** Remind yourself of your true identity—defined not by the setback but by God's unfailing love and commitment to your healing journey.
- **ADJUST THE STRATEGY:** Use insights from the setback to adjust your healing practices and establish stronger, healthier safeguards.

Your relapse does not define you. Instead, it provides crucial feedback, refining your path forward and deepening your reliance on God's unwavering grace.

RELAPSE DOESN'T GET THE LAST WORD

Maybe you've slipped. Maybe you've fallen back or glanced behind. Listen: You're not broken; you're human.

The crucial question isn't "Did you relapse?" It's "What will you remember next?" Now is the time to replace the lingering taste of Egypt—the slavery, garlic, leeks, onions, and meat—with the simple nourishment of manna. Yes, it might taste bland. Yes, it might lack the excitement of your past, but this manna is God's way of cleansing your palate, stabilizing your heart, and gently nourishing your soul.

The manna prepares us, steadies us, and aligns us to step boldly into the promised land—a place flowing with milk and honey, richness and abundance. This is the transition moment we're stepping into together as we look toward stage 3 of recovery: integration.

Relapse tries to convince us we've failed. But recovery boldly declares, "I choose again."

And, friend, hear me clearly: You absolutely can choose again. Together, we're walking into deeper healing, lasting freedom, and unshakable hope. Let's step forward into stage 3 with expectation and confidence, knowing the best is yet to come.

REFLECTION QUESTIONS

1. Are you rehearsing pain or remembering God's faithfulness?
2. Have you relapsed mentally, emotionally, or behaviorally?
3. Who in your circle may trigger old cravings?
4. What does manna—simple, steady provision—look like in your life right now?
5. What victory will you declare about your story today?

STAGE 3

INTEGRATION

You can now begin to work on decreasing shame and alienation, developing a greater capacity for healthy attachment, and taking up personal and professional goals that reflect post-traumatic meaning-making. Overcoming fears of normal life, healthy challenge and change, and intimacy become the focus of the work. As your life becomes reconsolidated around a healthy present and a healed self, the trauma feels farther away, part of an integrated understanding of self but no longer a daily focus.

—Janina Fisher[1]

18

RECONNECTION

We've reached the final, transformative stage of trauma recovery: integration.

This is the powerful space where the stories that once shattered us no longer control our present. The pain doesn't vanish completely, but, crucially, it no longer dominates our narrative. Instead, our experiences become threads woven into a richer, more complex tapestry of our life stories.

This stage is about reconnection—reconnecting deeply with our truths, our bodies, our communities, and, ultimately, God.

So let me ask, How are you? Have you been triggered reading this book? Have you found yourself in tears? Did certain chapters cause your stomach to drop or your heart to race? Have you needed to pause, go back, reread, or journal through moments?

If not, I encourage you to go back. Allow yourself to sit with those moments.

Not because I want to see you in pain but because confronting those moments head-on ensures that you'll finish this journey powerfully and authentically. When we courageously sit with our pain, we allow ourselves to metabolize it fully—transforming hurt into wisdom, strength, and emotional resilience. By metabolizing our pain, we integrate our experiences, which enables us to move through them rather than remain stuck within them, and eventually we get to a place of ownership over them.

This last stretch is about ownership:

Honoring your journey of healing
Attending carefully to any remaining areas needing attention

Let's get to work.

WHAT IS THE INNER CHILD?

You may have heard the term "inner child" and thought it sounded like New Age fluff. But that wasn't my reaction. The first time I heard it, something clicked. It didn't feel flaky—it felt freeing. It gave me language for something I had felt for a long time but didn't know how to explain. It helped me show grace and empathy to little Timmy—the boy in me who had endured pain long before he had words to name it.

My inner child is the part of me that experienced trauma before he understood what trauma even was. He's the one who figured out how to survive by hiding, pleasing, performing, fighting, or shutting down. He learned to protect me the only way he knew how. Not because he was weak but because he was wise enough to find a way to keep going.

And if I don't acknowledge him? He doesn't disappear—he takes the wheel.

When I'm reacting instead of responding? That's him.

When I'm isolating because I'm afraid of rejection? That's him.

When I'm angry and don't know why? That's him.

Either your inner child is walking with you in the present or you're still stuck in the past with your inner child. And the goal is not to silence that version of yourself. The goal is to integrate it. To welcome it into the light. To say, "I see you. You make sense. You're safe now." Connecting with our inner child isn't indulging weakness—it's practicing self-compassion, which is foundational for holistic healing.

That's how healing begins—when the adult version of you wraps arms around the younger version and says, "You're not alone anymore."

INTEGRATION MEANS YOUR PAST SELF IS NO LONGER CONTROLLING YOU

There's a saying: "Everywhere you go, there you are."

This truth should be written in Proverbs because it's so foundational. Yet many of us still try to outrun our past selves:

Working ourselves into exhaustion
Distracting ourselves with sex
Numbing ourselves with substances or entertainment
Endless scrolling or binge-watching
Overcommitting to social engagements
Obsessively seeking approval or validation

None of these methods work. In John 14:27, Jesus made it clear there is a peace the world offers—but it's temporary, fleeting, and unsatisfying. The peace He provides, in contrast, is lasting, deep, and authentic.

Our bodies hold every memory we've lived. Wherever we go, there we are—carrying everything we've ever been through, our entire histories, our deepest joys, and our lingering wounds. So we can't outrun those memories. But we can find our way to integration.

Integration, according to Janina Fisher, signifies that trauma no longer hijacks your present experience. It doesn't overwhelm your sleep, doesn't dominate your reactions, and doesn't plunge you into emotional chaos.

Trauma may still exist in your history—but it no longer dictates your day-to-day living. It's no longer running the show.

That's the reality I now inhabit. When memories of abuse or addiction or feelings of inadequacy surface, they feel distant—almost remote. They belong to a younger version of myself, a version I've grown to love, respect, and nurture rather than shame or criticize. Little Timmy survived the trauma of his past so that older Timmy could thrive despite it all.

But that younger self no longer holds the steering wheel. Truthfully, my older self doesn't either. The Holy Spirit is driving. I'm in the front passenger seat, fully trusting His direction. Little Timmy is safely seated right behind me, protected, cared for, and no longer controlling the journey.

Many mistakenly believe, "If I still remember it, I must not be healed."

That's simply not true.

True healing means that when memories return, we don't spiral out of control. When triggers arise, we recognize and name them. We choose a new, healthier response rather than falling back into old patterns.

This self-awareness demonstrates a safe mind and a regulated body.

TRIGGERED VS. AWARE

Before healing, triggers push us into harmful cycles: overthinking, taking things personally, isolating, acting out destructively. For me, this once looked like falling into cycles of pornography and masturbation. For others, it could be emotional eating, withdrawing from loved ones, or lashing out.

After healing, triggers still surface—but now I see them clearly in real time. I catch myself, reground, breathe, seek healthy connection, take walks, journal, talk openly with my wife, or play basketball—whatever adaptive behavior I need.

Integration and healing don't mean triggers vanish completely. Rather, healing empowers us with awareness and tools to manage them. It's vital to understand this clearly, especially if perfectionism tempts you to believe that recovery means you'll never face another trigger. Healing isn't about an absence of triggers; it's about developing the resilience and skills to manage them effectively. Your growth is evident not by never experiencing triggers again but by your changed responses when they inevitably arise.

Trauma might still linger in the background, but it no longer controls the narrative.

I don't want to exile little Timmy; I want to parent him with compassion and care. I want him to understand:

His body is safe.
His environment is stable.
His mind is at peace.

These were things he didn't experience growing up, and now, as an adult, I have the privilege and responsibility to provide them for him.

THE DOG DADDY

There's a real guy on YouTube called the Dog Daddy who rehabilitates reactive dogs using only a leash and his calm presence. He meets chaos with unwavering confidence. And, remarkably, the dogs respond positively, because even extreme reactivity can be rewired when calm, confident leadership is present.

This analogy illustrates precisely how I handle trauma now. It once dominated me, pulling me in every direction. Now when trauma surfaces, I confidently command it to "sit."

And let's be clear: I'm not trying to diss anybody, but every one of us has a little dog in us. Whether we're a Great Dane, a Chihuahua, a Labrador, a German shepherd, a golden retriever, or a French bulldog, each breed can exhibit reactivity and needs guidance. We all have internal instincts and reactions that need training, boundaries, and calm, consistent leadership to manage effectively.

That's not avoidance or dissociation—that's mastery. And I passionately want that for you too. When stress comes, we don't have to return to old coping mechanisms:

pornography
sugary binges
unnecessary fights
excessive drinking or substance use
endless distraction or busyness

Instead, we can manage that stress with real nourishment:

healthy, supportive relationships
peace through mindful daily practices
skills and disciplines developed over time

prayer, meditation, and spiritual connection
meaningful hobbies and physical activity

Healing has taught us how to practice patience with ourselves, how to self-soothe in healthy ways, and how to listen to what our bodies need. We no longer settle for emotional fast food—we choose substantial nourishment, authentic love, and genuine safety.

Integration is a beautiful part of the journey of recovery. It doesn't mean that you never cry, you never get triggered, or you never remember. It means that you're not controlled by it, you're not shocked when it shows up, you know how to return to peace, and you know how to reconnect—with God, with others, and with the younger version of you who needed safety. You know how to lead yourself with love.

And that, my friend, is the whole point.

REFLECTION QUESTIONS

1. How close does your trauma feel today?
2. When your inner child surfaces, do you shame or soothe?
3. What has integration looked like in your life?
4. Where do you still feel like you're falling back instead of moving forward?
5. What does reconnection mean to you, in this moment?

19

PRESS ON

I used to read Philippians 3:12–14 like a motivational speech: *I press on . . . I forget what's behind . . . I reach toward the prize.* But when I revisited this passage during the journey of writing this book, it landed differently—not because Paul changed, but because I did.

After living through trauma, after doing the deep, relentless soul work of healing and integration, I've found that Scripture hits differently. It stops sounding like a spiritual checklist and becomes more like a map guiding me toward emotional and spiritual wholeness.

Paul wrote clearly, "I don't mean to say that I have already achieved these things. . . . But I press on to possess that perfection for which Christ Jesus first possessed me. . . . I focus on this one thing: Forgetting the past and looking forward to what lies ahead" (Phil. 3:12–13 NLT).

This isn't perfectionism—it's perseverance. It's trauma-informed theology at its best.

Why trauma informed? Because Paul explicitly acknowledged the past without allowing it to define the present or future. His words demonstrate healthy emotional regulation, recognizing where he'd been without being trapped there. He exemplified forward movement—pursuing wholeness while being grounded in the secure identity given him by Christ rather than staying stuck in regret or shame. This is trauma-informed theology at its best because it validates the journey of healing while steadfastly pointing toward growth and restoration.

WHAT IS YOUR PRESS?

Let's get practical.

"Press" is both an action and an anchor. It's your determination—the reason you push through hard days, the flame that keeps burning when life feels overwhelming.

Your press needs a name, something deeply personal and uniquely meaningful to you. Maybe your press is being free, breaking generational cycles, finding purpose, or reclaiming dignity. My press? It's peace. That's why I wrote this book—peace is my action and my anchor. Every day I wake up grateful for the peace of God, the peace that "surpasses all understanding," guarding my heart and mind through Christ Jesus (Phil. 4:7). I'm committed to protecting and nurturing the peace the Prince of Peace provides. That's my press, my unwavering determination.

If you don't have a clear press, your healing journey will falter when adversity strikes. You'll relapse into old habits because, truthfully, this journey is long. Grace carries you, but it's your press that moves you forward.

Having a press isn't about hustle culture or toxic productivity. It's about alignment—showing up consistently with honesty, compassion, and grit. Paul experienced revelations, even visits to the third heaven, yet he still declared, "I press" (Phil. 3:14). Knowing Jesus doesn't exempt you from recovery; it equips you for it.

This alignment means understanding that pressing forward doesn't come from striving endlessly or chasing external validation—it's rooted in the steady, honest commitment to who God created you to be. Paul's press was anchored in his divine calling, not his circumstances. His revelations didn't exempt him from trials; rather, they provided clarity and conviction to endure them.

I've walked thirty years of faith alongside twenty-eight years of therapy, and I'm still pressing. Some mornings I still feel heavy, but every day I choose to breathe, pray, and press forward. Healing isn't a singular event; it's a lifestyle commitment—a daily choice to move forward, anchored by grace and guided by divine strength.

SPRINTS COLLAPSE, MARATHONS SUSTAIN

Even as we choose to press every day, it won't always be easy or even successful.

Short-term efforts collapse under long-term pressures. I've witnessed people press briefly—begin therapy, join church groups—full of initial enthusiasm and fervor, committed to transforming their lives. They're like runners eagerly sprinting from the starting line, energized, vibrant, and confident. But then the first sign of discomfort arises—the initial wave of emotional exhaustion, the minor inconvenience of scheduling conflicts, or the deeper challenge of confronting a painful memory. Suddenly they're stopping, bowing out quietly, and retreating back into old patterns. Months later, the unresolved pain roars back louder, stronger, and more entrenched.

Think about sprinters. Their bodies are built for explosive speed, muscular and powerful, capable of stunning performances over short distances. Yet put those same sprinters into a marathon and the impressive muscle that propelled them in the short term will quickly become a hindrance. Marathon runners, on the other hand, aren't muscular powerhouses; they're lean, enduring, and steady. Their strength isn't showy or explosive; it's rooted deep within, built through persistent training, dedication, and a relentless commitment to the long haul.

Healing, likewise, is not a sprint—it's a marathon, a steady journey of sustained effort, emotional resilience, and deep-rooted patience. Jesus runs this marathon with you, matching your pace, guiding your steps, ensuring that you endure until the finish line.

PRESS FOR YOURSELF

In my struggle with addiction, every relapse felt like a failure not just to myself but also to Juliette. I initially pressed forward motivated by her reactions, her disappointment, and the fear of losing her. I was determined to stop my maladaptive behaviors to protect my marriage, keep her happy, and fulfill the image of the husband she deserved. But here's the reality I had to face head-on: External motivations—even as powerful as love—won't sustain genuine, long-term healing.

One day, clarity struck like lightning. As much as I cherished Juliette, my healing couldn't be contingent upon her presence. If she left or even if she stayed, my motivation couldn't rise and fall with her emotional response to me. It had to come from within. I had to want freedom and peace for me—independent of any relationship or external validation. My press needed to be rooted in my identity, not in codependency or temporary satisfaction of external expectations.

I finally understood that my deepest press wasn't about becoming a better husband, a better pastor, or even a better believer—it was about becoming the man God always created me to be: a free man, a peaceful man. And when I say "peaceful," I don't simply mean calm—I mean literally full of peace.

The Prince of Peace Himself gives me this peace as a gift, a peace so deep and profound that it leaves no room for the chaos of old habits or maladaptive behaviors. When I am committed to staying full of His peace, there's simply no space for anything else. This transformative peace guides every decision, anchors me through storms, and keeps my feet firmly planted on the path of healing.

This personal press—this unshakable peace—is what sustains me.

BREAKING CYCLES

Paul said clearly, "When I was a child, I spoke and thought and reasoned as a child. But when I grew up, I put away childish things" (1 Cor. 13:11 NLT).

Many trauma responses were survival tactics from childhood. They were protective mechanisms—emotional armor that shielded us from overwhelming pain or danger. Perhaps as a child, withdrawing emotionally kept you safe in chaotic homes. Being overly compliant might have prevented explosive reactions from caregivers. Hypervigilance could have offered a sense of control in unpredictable environments. Anger or aggression might have created necessary boundaries when none were respected. Let's honor our younger selves for their creativity and resilience. They did the best they could with limited resources and understanding.

Yet today these same tactics stunt our emotional and relational growth. Emotional withdrawal now prevents intimacy. Compliance leads to lost authenticity and resentment. Hypervigilance exhausts our nervous systems and robs us of peace. Unchecked anger isolates us from meaningful connections. To thrive, we must mature—press upward. Growth requires us to shed outdated strategies and courageously embrace healthier ways of being.

What's your press? It needs to be resilient:

If they stay, I press.
If they leave, I press.
If I'm hired, I press.
If I'm fired, I press.
If I'm celebrated, I press.
If I'm misunderstood, I press.

RECOGNIZING DISTRACTIONS

Oppression, depression, repression, suppression—these emotional states are strategic distractions designed to derail your press. Oppression weighs us down externally, stealing our hope and vision. Depression clouds our minds, saps our strength, and leaves us feeling stuck. Repression buries vital truths, creating emotional land mines that later explode. Suppression blocks our voices, keeping essential healing conversations at bay.

The Enemy doesn't have to destroy you; he only needs to discourage your perseverance. But here's the powerful truth: You have the power to remove these negative prefixes.

Replace oppression with freedom. Seek support and actively fight back against limiting beliefs.

Overcome depression by engaging in healthy connections, routines, and therapy.

Address repression through courageous self-exploration and guided healing.

Break suppression by finding safe spaces and trusted people to express yourself authentically.

Remove these negative prefixes from your life—just press.

Initially, pressing forward in the face of distractions will feel exhausting, much like exercising after a prolonged sedentary lifestyle. The first days of working out bring soreness, fatigue, and doubts about your capacity to continue. But with persistence, muscles strengthen, endurance increases, and what once felt overwhelmingly difficult soon becomes routine and empowering. Similarly, emotional and spiritual healing builds its own muscle memory.

Over time, your soul remembers healthier rhythms. Your emotional resilience strengthens, your spiritual insight deepens, and even tough days transform into sacred opportunities for growth. Your heart learns to confidently whisper, "This is the day the Lord has made. I will rejoice."

MOVING FORWARD

When Juliette and I do counseling sessions for other people, we provide empathy and support, and then we challenge. Think of us like instructors during Navy SEAL training. We're there to instruct, guide, and support—but we can't run after you if you decide to ring the bell and tap out. If individuals continually rehearse their pain without implementing any strategies or practical steps we've shared, we lovingly release them. Not because we don't care but because healing and growth demand action, courage, and commitment. They require us to press.

Staying stuck eventually becomes a choice. This is not a judgment but an invitation. It's an invitation to something better, something healthier, something powerful. You don't have to remain trapped in pain, endlessly replaying old wounds. It's time to get up. You can do it. You can take that next step. You can push for one more rep, one more breath, one more courageous decision. It's not easy, but it's absolutely worth it.

I continue to press myself, not because my trauma has vanished or because life suddenly became perfect. No, I press because I have discovered that God remains steadfastly beside me in every moment of tension. I press because peace isn't passive—it's waiting on the other side of courageous movement. My healing—just like yours—is valuable, worthy of every ounce of effort, every moment of discomfort, and every brave step forward.

Your life's call is so much louder, so much more profound than your trauma's echo. So rise. Press forward. You've got this, because you were created for more.

REFLECTION QUESTIONS

1. What ignites your inner fire to press forward?
2. Are you building healthy rhythms or simply sprinting in recovery?
3. Which distractions threaten your perseverance?
4. What practical step will you take to press today?
5. Who will you become because you chose to press forward?

20

KEEP MOVING FORWARD

There are some parts of recovery that simply aren't optional.

At some point, I have to choose.

Choose to start.

Choose to stay.

Choose to keep going when it gets uncomfortable.

Healing doesn't happen by accident or coincidence. I didn't just wake up one day free from anxiety or trauma, nor did peace just casually stroll into my life. I consciously chose it. I actively stepped into a regulated nervous system through intentional daily practices and purposeful effort. Peace didn't find me—I went looking for it, pursued it, and created space for it.

Choosing means making daily decisions even when my feelings don't align, even when comfort pulls me backward. It's an active, courageous choice every single morning to embrace peace, healing, and wholeness on purpose.

THE POWER OF CHOOSING TO FORGET

Let's keep working through Paul's words in his letter to the church at Philippi: "I focus on this one thing: Forgetting the past and looking forward to what lies ahead, I press on" (Phil. 3:13–14 NLT).

Forgetting isn't amnesia.

It's not dissociation.

It's not spiritual bypassing.

It's an intentional decision.

The Greek word that Paul used for "forgetting" literally means "no longer paying attention to." It carries the weight of actively deactivating something in our minds—not erasing it, but deliberately repositioning it. Paul wasn't advocating denial; he was providing permission—permission to consciously shift focus from what previously imprisoned us toward what now frees us.

The issue with forgetting is that sometimes we are still in love with our old flesh. The way we talk about the old us is romanticized. I hear it sometimes in the church: "Back in the day, man, I used to be wild. I used to be tough. I used to . . ."

Why are we talking about our dysfunction like it deserves nostalgia? That version of me nearly killed me because it kept me trapped in cycles of destructive behavior. That version of me lost people because it prioritized short-term thrills over lasting relationships. That version of me lived in bondage because it didn't understand the freedom available through grace.

I don't need to romanticize the brokenness or maintain an unhealthy attachment to the chaos that once defined me. Doing that would be like having an affair with my past while trying to pursue my freedom. I can't be committed to healing and still flirt with dysfunction.

I need to celebrate the grace that pulled me out. If I romanticize my dysfunction, I deny myself the healing I need.

Some of us don't struggle with romanticizing the past so much as being able to leave the guilt behind. But let's look to Paul again. He once persecuted Christians. Imprisoned them. Oversaw executions. This man didn't just oppose the faith—he terrorized it. He was by our modern definition a religious extremist. A persecutor turned preacher. A threat turned theologian.

Imagine trying to plant churches knowing you murdered some of the very people who would've led them. Picture walking into a room filled with the loved ones of your past victims and saying, "Follow me as I follow Christ."

That's the tension Paul lived in. That's the weight he carried—but somehow he didn't let that weight crush him. And here's what wrecks me: He gave himself permission to be new. He didn't just preach 2 Corinthians 5:17—"If anyone is in Christ, he is a new creation"—he lived it. He *embodied* it. He had to.

Because if he hadn't? If he had let guilt keep the mic? If shame had become his spiritual GPS? Then we never would have gotten Romans. We never would have gotten Ephesians. We never would have heard about being saved . . . If Paul had stayed stuck in who he was, we would have lost out on the fullness of who he became.

He had to forget—not because what he did didn't matter but because what God was doing mattered more. He had to forget—not to erase his past but to walk fully into his purpose. He had to hold on to grace tighter than guilt. That's the only way forward. And that's not just Paul's story—it's ours.

THE CONJUNCTION THAT CHANGED EVERYTHING

"I focus on this one thing: forgetting the past *and* looking forward" (Phil 3:13).

That "and" is critical. Don't miss it. Put it in bold. Put it in quotes. Frame it. Because that one conjunction flips the whole thing.

It sounds like two separate actions—forgetting and looking forward—but Paul called it *one thing.* Why? Because these movements are connected. Inseparable. Siamese twins of the soul.

If I don't forget, I can't look forward. If I'm not looking forward, I haven't truly let go of the past. That little word "and" carries the weight of healing. It's a bridge. A hinge. A holy intersection where grace meets motion.

That's why it's one of the most profound conjunctions in all of Scripture. It ties together two spiritual actions and makes them one practice. Like peanut butter and jelly. Like healing and hope. Like grace and grit.

This is how Paul kept pushing. He held both at once—letting go while leaning in. Releasing what was behind and reaching toward what was ahead. Not perfect. Not polished. But in motion. Always in motion.

I forget and I press forward. I perpetually have hope for the future. If you're in a relationship with Christ and if you're pursuing your mental health, you are constantly being called forward. What did Jesus spend His ministry saying to the disciples? "Follow Me." In other words, "Keep coming closer to Me. Keep moving forward."

Some days, healing is loud. Breakthroughs hit like thunder. Revelation strikes. Tears cleanse. Hope rises like a flood. But other days? Healing is quiet. Subtle. Almost invisible. Here's something I want you to remember. Even when it feels like you went forward only an inch, you moved. Whether you took a big leap or a medium-sized step, or you just went one inch forward, you moved forward.

Progress doesn't always look like a leap. Sometimes it's a step. Sometimes it's a half step. Sometimes it's just a decision not to go backward to what broke you. That, too, is progress.

It's deciding to get out of bed. To pray again. To show up when you'd rather disappear. To stay in the process.

Progress is rarely linear. Healing curves, twists, doubles back. Some seasons are silent. Others erupt with growth. But every moment you keep walking—even with a limp—is a moment that matters.

Don't despise the inch. Don't discount the slow days. Some of the most powerful transformations are happening deep below the surface. So we need to keep looking forward to tomorrow. We need to keep pressing, one small step at a time.

I wake up in the morning not knowing whether this is going to be my best day or my worst day. All I know is I still have the King of glory inside me, and there's nothing I face that He won't help me navigate through. I look forward to my days and what the future holds. I look forward to what God wants to do and where He wants to take me, because I know every day I'm moving closer to Him.

HOLD ON TO THE PROGRESS

Paul wrote, "We must hold on to the progress we have already made" (Phil. 3:16 NLT).

Hold on. Grip it. Don't let it slide. This isn't just a spiritual encouragement—it's a *strategy* for survival. Holding on is active. Intentional. It means protecting your growth, even when you're tired. It's like wearing a retainer after braces.

I wore braces for two years. Two years of painful, slow, awkward transformation. I followed all the rules. I brushed after every meal. I avoided candy and soda. I wanted that smile to be right when the brackets came off. And when they *finally* came off, my orthodontist handed me a plastic case. Inside? A retainer.

It looked like a mini version of the very thing I just got free from. It annoyed me. Made me drool. I was fourteen or fifteen—self-conscious and sick of slobber. So I did what a lot of people do. I stopped wearing it.

Fast-forward a year. My dad said it's time to go back for a checkup. I panicked. I tore up my room looking for that blue case. I finally found it under my bed, caked in dust like a buried time capsule.

I rinsed it off. Popped it into my mouth. And instantly—*pop*—it sprang right back out.

It didn't fit. I hadn't even felt my teeth shift. I hadn't noticed the regression. But the evidence was in my mouth. All that slow progress was slipping—because I didn't protect it.

And that's what Paul's words are warning us about. Hold on to what you've gained. Don't assume progress will keep itself. Transformation has to be *tended to*. If not, regression happens silently. Subtly. Then one day what used to fit—freedom, peace, clarity—doesn't sit right anymore.

You won't even feel the drift until it's already happened. That's why spiritual retainers matter. The practices, the habits, the boundaries—they may not feel flashy. But they're how we *hold the line*.

Keep praying. Keep journaling. Keep going to therapy. Keep coming to community. Keep setting those healthy boundaries. Keep reminding yourself of who you are now. You've come too far to lose what's been reshaped.

Jesus did the initial work. He realigned our hearts. He took our sin, our shame, our trauma and reset everything. Not partially. Completely. He didn't just forgive us—He *shifted* us. Like braces on crooked teeth, He applied the pressure of grace and love until our hearts aligned with the righteousness of God.

That's what Scripture means when it says we've been made new (2 Cor. 5:17). We didn't slowly morph into righteousness—we were declared righteous by the finished work of Jesus. Our position changed in an instant, even if our process takes a lifetime.

But that initial shift isn't the end. Because alignment doesn't always hold by itself. Enter the Holy Spirit. The Holy Spirit is the

Retainer. He keeps us from drifting back to dysfunction. He holds the new shape. He doesn't scream. He whispers. *You can't go back there. That behavior won't serve you anymore. You're healed now. Let's keep moving.*

He isn't just a vibe or a goose bump. He's a *regulator*. He's the internal bracing that tells your spirit, "That doesn't fit anymore." And when you start to shift, you *feel* it. You sense the tension. That's the Spirit at work.

And here's the good news: It's not shame—it's love. He's not guilting you into goodness. He's *guarding* your growth.

Jesus adjusted you. The Spirit retains you. One aligns. The other sustains. One shifted your story. The other preserves your progress.

You're not in this alone. Heaven didn't just fix you and walk away. You were graced *and* given guidance.

YOU'RE NOT WHO YOU WERE

The cross wasn't easy for Jesus. But He endured it. Not because He was focused on the pain but because He saw *past* it.

He saw joy. He saw resurrection. He saw reunion. He saw *you*.

And He invites you to do the same. Look past the pain. Past the grief. Past the trauma. Past the relapse. Past the cycle. And see the *future*.

Because you're not who you were. You're not what you did. You're not what was done to you. You're not the name they called you. You're not the worst version of yourself.

You're redeemed. You're becoming. You're breaking free. Every inch forward proves it.

So I'll ask you—what are you looking forward to? Not what are you dreading? Not what are you afraid of? What are you *hoping* for?

Start there. Move toward *that*. Even if it's one inch at a time.

You've exhausted your past. You already know what that looks like. But what's ahead? What haven't you seen yet? What haven't you done? What are you dreaming about that still feels scary—but holy?

Let's go into the unknown—not with fear, but with *faith*. We're not stuck in trauma anymore. We're not scared of the future. We're not afraid to fail.

We've got vision now. We've got forward motion now. We've got God *with us* now.

So let's go get it. Let's go build something we've never seen. Let's go touch healing we've never felt. Let's go walk in purpose we didn't think was possible.

One inch at a time. One step at a time. But always forward.

Let's move.

REFLECTION QUESTIONS

1. Is your progress collecting dust?
2. What would it look like to pick up your "retainer" and hold your alignment?
3. What past moment have you been romanticizing instead of releasing?
4. What does forward look like for you right now?
5. What are you looking forward to?

CONCLUSION

If you made it to the end of this book, I want to pause and honor the courage that got you here.

I'm not a therapist. I'm a man who's been through trauma, walked the healing road, and stayed in therapy long enough to know this work never really ends—it just shifts. It gets gentler. Less jagged. More rooted.

I hope the Holy Spirit has held you in the hard places. I hope you've seen yourself in these pages, not with shame, but with compassion. And I hope that at some point along the way, you reached out for help. Maybe to a friend. Maybe to a pastor. Maybe, finally, to a therapist.

That alone is a miracle.

This book is my attempt to normalize conversations we've kept hidden for too long—especially in the church. I wrote it because I was tired of watching leaders fall while congregations flinched. I was tired of silence being mistaken for strength. I was tired of trauma being dismissed, demonized, or ignored.

Because here's what I know: Unspoken pain becomes secret shame. Untended trauma becomes a public tragedy. What we refuse to name will eventually name us.

So I want to see something different: a church that can hold honest stories. Leaders who model transparency. Communities that don't flinch when someone says, "I'm not okay."

Because when people fall, it's rarely about lust. Or pills. Or pride. It's trauma. Trauma that went unspoken, unprocessed, and unshared. Sometimes—yes—it's sin. But sin doesn't just show up out of nowhere. We were born in sin, shaped in iniquity. Most sin is rooted in pain. In unhealed wounds. In trauma.

What if people just said this instead?

"I'm tempted. I need help."
"I'm spiraling. I need a break."
"I'm not strong right now. Please pray for me."

It would change everything. We wouldn't have to rebuild so many broken churches. We wouldn't have to reconcile so many shattered relationships.

Because healing isn't about appearing perfect. It's about being honest enough to get healthy.

Paul didn't hide his thorn. He named it. He didn't hide his weakness. He wrote about it in his letters and called it grace. That's the model. And I refuse to lead any other way.

Not for my wife.

Not for my sons.

Not for my friends.

Not even for myself.

I want to be whole.

I want stability. I want peace. And I want it for you too. But I can't want it more than you do. So if you're ready to commit—if you're ready to build a life that isn't ruled by the past—I want to invite you to fall in love with the Master's peace. And then protect it like it's sacred.

Because it is. Don't rush past this moment. Sit in it. Let it settle. Let it breathe. Take one more deep breath and remember: God is not in a hurry with your healing.

You have time.

You have space.

You have grace.

And if all you can do today is whisper, "God, help me keep going," that's enough.

You're not behind. You're not disqualified. You're not alone. You're becoming.

Let me pray for you before you go.

Holy Spirit, thank You for every person who picked up this book. Whether they read one chapter or all of them, I ask that You meet them in their honesty. I pray they become safe people who create safe places. May they live fully seen, fully heard, fully known, and fully loved. And may they protect their peace until it overflows. In Jesus's name, amen.

ACKNOWLEDGMENTS

Writing a book is never a solo endeavor, and this one is no exception. There are a few people I need to thank—people whose encouragement, patience, and expertise helped bring *The Missing Peace* into existence.

First, Andrew Stoddard—you saw something in this book before I did. You encouraged me to write this book instead of the one I originally planned, and looking back, I see the wisdom in that push. Thank you for redirecting me toward what needed to be written.

To Sydnie Shreffler—the friendliest and most patient ghost I could ever ask for. Casper has nothing on you! Your skill, kindness, and ability to handle my words with care made this journey so much smoother. I'm beyond grateful. And the truth is, even though I ultimately rewrote your draft, I couldn't have written what I did without the foundation you laid. You helped me find the shape of this book.

Jessica Rogers—you have the patience of Job. I know I had to be getting on your nerves with how all over the place I was, but somehow you still understood me. Your ability to take my scattered thoughts and bring them together? That's a gift. And you, my friend, are dope.

Natalie Nyquist—you got this book through the maternity ward and into the hands of readers. Thank you for carrying it across the finish line with care and excellence. I appreciate you more than words can say.

Dr. Anita Phillips—my Dr. Sister. You helped me clarify my thoughts and words to make sure I wasn't misrepresenting the mental health professionals I deeply respect. Your insight was invaluable, and I will always be grateful for your wisdom and guidance.

Dr. Jenna Mountain—aka Captain Marvel—you challenged me to ensure that this book wasn't just spiritually grounded but also clinically sound. You pushed me to make sure this wasn't just a book *about* healing but one that was trauma informed in its bones. That challenge changed everything.

Dr. Stephanie Thurston-Simmons—you graciously read through this manuscript more than once, offering invaluable clinical context and language that helped bring clarity and safety to the words. Your generosity made a real difference in this final product. Thank you.

To everyone who played a part in making this book a reality—thank you. I pray this book serves you, challenges you, and brings you the peace you need.

With gratitude,
Tim

NOTES

INTRODUCTION: SOMETHING AIN'T RIGHT

1. "COVID-19 Pandemic Triggers 25% Increase in Prevalence of Anxiety and Depression Worldwide," World Health Organization, March 2, 2022, https://www.who.int/news/item/02-03-2022-covid-19-pandemic-triggers-25-increase-in-prevalence-of-anxiety-and-depression-worldwide.
2. Kirsi Auro et al., "Attention-Deficit/Hyperactivity Disorder Diagnoses in Finland During the COVID-19 Pandemic," *JAMA Network Open* 7, no. 6 (2024): e2418204, https://doi.org/10.1001/jamanetworkopen.2024.18204.
3. "New APA Poll: One in Three Americans Feels Lonely Every Week," American Psychiatric Association, January 30, 2024, https://www.psychiatry.org/news-room/news-releases/new-apa-poll-one-in-three-americans-feels-lonely-e.
4. Thomas B. Folino et al., "Propofol," NCBI Bookshelf, last updated July 24, 2023, https://www.ncbi.nlm.nih.gov/books/NBK430884/.

CHAPTER 1: WHAT AM I MISSING?

1. Benjamin A. Swerdlow et al., "Maladaptive Behavior and Affect Regulation: A Functionalist Perspective," *Emotion* 20, no. 1 (2020): 75–79, https://doi.org/10.1037/emo0000660.

CHAPTER 3: CRY ME A RIVER

1. "What Is Bile Duct Cancer?," National Cancer Institute, last updated May 15, 2024, https://www.cancer.gov/types/liver/bile-duct-cancer.
2. "Cancer Stat Facts: Liver and Intrahepatic Bile Duct Cancer," National Cancer Institute, accessed January 29, 2025, https://seer.cancer.gov/statfacts/html/livibd.html.
3. Reena Mukamal, "All About Emotional Tears," American Academy of Ophthalmology, February 28, 2017, https://www.aao.org/eye-health/tips-prevention/all-about-emotional-tears.
4. "The Power of Tears," Wesson & Mothershed Eye Center, April 21, 2020, https://www.wandmeyes.com/the-power-of-tears/.

CHAPTER 4: A FIRE OF WORDS

1. "Trauma-Informed Stabilization Treatment," Janina Fisher, accessed August 20, 2025, https://janinafisher.com/tist/.

CHAPTER 6: TURN ON THE LIGHTS

1. Prahlad Yeri, "Does the Theory That 'Sincerely' Originated from 'Without Wax' Hold Any Merit?," English Language & Usage, Stack Exchange, August 19, 2016, https://english.stackexchange.com/questions/343644/does-the-theory-that-sincerely-originated-from-without-wax-hold-any-merit.

CHAPTER 10: UNSPOKEN

1. Jeff Wallenfeldt, "Silent Generation," *Encyclopedia Britannica*, last updated January 13, 2025, https://www.britannica.com/topic/Silent-Generation.

CHAPTER 11: HOW DO I START TALKING WHEN IT FEELS IMPOSSIBLE?

1. Matthew D. Lieberman et al., "Putting Feelings into Words," *Psychological Science* 18, no. 5 (2007): 421–28, https://doi.org/10

.1111/j.1467-9280.2007.01916.x; Bessel van der Kolk, *The Body Keeps the Score: Brain, Mind, and Body in the Healing of Trauma* (Viking, 2014).

2. Alejandra O'Connell-Domenech, "Why More Americans Are Going to Therapy," *The Hill*, May 1, 2023, https://thehill.com/policy/healthcare/3975996-why-more-americans-are-going-to-therapy/.

STAGE 1: SAFETY AND STABILIZATION

1. Janina Fisher, "3 Stages of Trauma Recovery," Unfinished Conversation, accessed January 29, 2025, https://unfinishedconversation.com/resources/3-stages-of-trauma-recovery-uc-handout/.

CHAPTER 14: SAFE MIND

1. Cathy Dimarchos, "The Science Behind Paying Attention: How Focus Shapes Your Reality," *Business, Culture & Leadership Insights* (blog), Solutions2You, January 14, 2025, https://www.solutions2you.com.au/blog/the-science-behind-paying-attention.

STAGE 2: REMEMBRANCE

1. Fisher, "3 Stages of Trauma Recovery."

STAGE 3: INTEGRATION

1. Fisher, "3 Stages of Trauma Recovery."

ABOUT THE AUTHOR

Tim Ross, bestselling author and host of the popular podcasts *The Basement* and *Wide Open*, was born in Inglewood, California, and went to college to study administration of justice to become a law enforcement officer. But God had other plans: Tim gave his life to Jesus Christ on January 14, 1996, and he started preaching on February 25, 1996. He's been walking with Jesus ever since. In June of 1997, he moved to Dallas, and in the time he's spent in the great state of Texas, Tim served in several ministry capacities, including youth evangelist, young adult pastor, director of student ministries, associate campus pastor, executive pastor of apostolic ministries, and lead pastor. Tim now occupies his time as a podcaster, social media influencer, bestselling author, and preacher.